SUPER
CONNECTOR

SUPER
CONNECTOR

STOP
NETWORKING
AND START
BUILDING BUSINESS
RELATIONSHIPS
THAT MATTER

SCOTT GERBER & RYAN PAUGH

Da Capo
LIFE
LONG

Da Capo Press
Hachette Book Group
1290 Avenue of the Americas, New York, NY 10104
www.dacapopress.com
@DaCapoPress

Printed in the United States of America

First Edition: February 2018

Published by Da Capo Press, an imprint of Perseus Books, LLC, a subsidiary of Hachette Book Group, Inc. The Da Capo Press name and logo is a trademark of the Hachette Book Group.

The Hachette Speakers Bureau provides a wide range of authors for speaking events. To find out more, go to www.hachettespeakersbureau.com or call (866) 376-6591.

The publisher is not responsible for websites (or their content) that are not owned by the publisher.

Print book interior design by Amy Quinn

Library of Congress Control Number: 2017953710

ISBNs: 978-0-7382-1996-7 (hardcover); 978-0-7382-1997-4 (ebook)

LSC-C

10 9 8 7 6 5 4 3 2 1

CONTENTS

FOREWORD

By Keith Ferrazzi

When I first published *Never Eat Alone* in 2005, having a PalmPilot and a BlackBerry was state of the art, social media was a choice between Facebook or MySpace, and "networking" was how you got ahead. "It's not what you know; it's who you know" was a popular corporate mantra, leading countless thirsty junior executives to brush up on their conversational skills or attend a seminar to learn the tricks to successful "networking." I was lucky, though: I had the best "networking coach" around—my father, Pete. Like most immigrant parents, he raised me to show up early, learn everything I could, work hard, and be of service. Through him, I learned that it mattered not how many people you knew but how many people you helped, because those were the people who would be there for you when *you* needed help.

I wrote *Never Eat Alone* because I saw that the way people networked was all wrong. The standard approach was transactional and self-interested, with the guiding principle being "What can this person do for me?" There was no sincerity, no authenticity, just a desire to grab as many business cards as possible, in the hopes that one day one of them would produce a return. Coming from an Italian family, this made no sense to me. Community is a driving force in Italian culture, and you can't create a community if everyone is just looking out for themselves. You need to look out for each other, develop opportunities for others, and find ways to make sure you all succeed: as the saying goes, a rising tide lifts all boats.

Of course, knowing what to do and knowing *how* to do it are rarely the same thing. Telling people "Be generous, be sincere, be authentic" can sound more like "Put yourself out there, and open yourself up to ridicule and humiliation," and no one wants that. It was always easier to have a game face, but "game face" is just a euphemism for "mask." I wanted to introduce the idea of leading with generosity, of showing how what you bring to the table can benefit others, and how creating a network means reaching out and being generous not just with your immediate circle of friends, but with acquaintances who may not share your interests but have complementary skills and expertise. By taking care of the people within your sphere of influence, they, in turn, will take care of you.

The development of social networks over the past decade has made forming those initial connections easier. A click of a button and you're officially someone's "follower"; two clicks and you're "friends." It's the twenty-first-century version of collecting business cards. But even with all this immediate connectivity to almost anyone, the mechanics of forming those relationships hasn't changed: we still want to know each other as individuals, not just as job titles; we still want to work with people we like and who have our best interests in mind; and mostly, we want to connect and partner with people with an interest in not only their own success but the success of others as well.

Being a Superconnector isn't a talent or a gift—it's having the awareness to realize that we all want the same things, even if we take different paths. It's reaching out to someone else and saying, "I can help you get there." It's having the generosity of spirit that would never reduce success to a zero-sum game. Seeing people like Scott and Ryan take my words to heart and expand on them by developing their own approaches to connecting instead of networking has been gratifying. While technology is constantly changing and improving to help us become more connected with others, it can't improve upon one person's offer of support and generosity to another. Books like this remind us that it will always be the human connection to helping each other that matters most.

SUPERCONNECTIONS

This is a book about building relationships. Relationships that exist for mutual benefit. Relationships through which something wonderful can happen. It is a book about community, and community building, and the very real need for connection. It is a book for anyone looking to enhance his or her relationship-making ability, both professionally and personally.

Relationship building is something that we take very seriously. Our entire professional lives have been based on helping business owners, entrepreneurs, and professionals meaningfully connect and build value with one another. We pride ourselves on our expertise in this area, and over the years we have developed a strong methodology for how to go about building, fostering, nurturing, developing, and maintaining relationships.

We want to help you understand the power of connection, too. As the world gets noisier and busier, connecting has never been more important. The next generation of success via social capital will be determined by those who have walled-off access to the people who matter.

We want to help you become the sort of person who has that kind of access. To be a connector.

A *Superconnector.*

Superconnectors are a new category of tradespeople born out of the social media era. They are highly valuable community builders who make things happen through their keen understanding and utilization of social capital—that is, the people you meet and the standing you have with them. We believe that social capital is the most important currency in the world. People, not money, are your most important assets; great things in business happen when the right people come together.

"Superconnectors are people who just seem to know everyone," says Keith Ferrazzi, the founder of Ferrazzi Greenlight, a research and consulting firm, who actually coined the term *Superconnector* in his landmark book, *Never Eat Alone.* Ferrazzi says these people appreciate the importance of "weak ties" as well as strong relationships. To expand your range of interests and expertise, Ferrazzi explains, you need to diversify your network and incorporate people with whom you have less in common but whose interests are complementary. And Superconnectors connect with a whole spectrum of people.

Superconnectors are information brokers. Their power comes from what they know just as much as whom they know. Obviously, the two are not mutually exclusive; Superconnectors are constantly learning and constantly connecting. They know that the more right people you meet, the more you learn, and vice versa. This is also one of the reasons people are attracted to this type of connector: in a noisy world, that's a one-two punch.

Superconnectors can do what they do because they understand the essence of community building, that is, the process of connecting people for mutual gain. They are patient, knowing that long-term gains trump short-term ones. The rewards they reap might not be evident for years to come, but that's not an issue. Superconnectors play the long game. They have patience and dedication. (In Aesop parlance, they would be the tortoise.)

To that end, Superconnectors aren't born. You can learn to be a Superconnector (which is exactly what this book is about!). You might think that Superconnectors are extroverted and love to be the life of the party, but not always. In fact, some of the best connectors we know are serious introverts who became Superconnectors in spite of—or, perhaps, because of—their introversion. They get lost at big events. They shine in smaller one-on-one interactions. They create opportunities to connect with people who fit their unique style of relationship building.

But Superconnectors don't meet others for the sake of amassing a museum-worthy collection of business cards. Superconnectors care about people, and they love connecting people who should be connected. They understand the power of relationship building, and they purposefully bring people or groups together with the intention to create mutual value. They are emotionally intelligent and empathetic. They understand how to uncover the needs and desires of those they aim to connect, even if those people don't clearly know what they're looking for themselves.

True relationship building is a master craft that takes tremendous time, energy, and thought. (A maxim: Anybody can call themselves a connector; only others can call you a Superconnector.)

"We all love an overnight success story, but behind every overnight success story that's endured you'll see lots of internal work, a lot of thinking and preparation that no one knows about," says author Shane Snow, the cofounder of Contently. "The difference between a one-hit wonder and someone who goes on to have a career is that the latter has done more work that no one has seen. It's not just luck that they hit the charts—there's a lot of planning and recognition. It's the same thing, whether it's making music or being a connector. The best ones have done the prep work."

In an age when we are all desperate for instant gratification (and many people do still really want to believe that there is a five-minute-abs formula for building a professional network—not to mention ab building), it's easy for unoriginal posers to continue to regurgitate jargon-laden, one-size-fits-all tidbits to advance their own self-interest. This false narrative has continued to push the notion that being "connected" and being a "connector" are the same thing to millions of people.

Nothing could be further from the truth. And in the long run, only one of those mind-sets will offer any real pathway to relationship-building success. Guess which one that is? That's right. The connector.

WHY YOU SHOULD LISTEN TO ANYTHING WE HAVE TO SAY

Because the two of us have lived exactly what we are preaching.

We were introduced in 2010 through a mutual friend, Dan Schawbel, who's made a big name for himself as an expert on millennials and the workplace. We each knew Schawbel through our own individual channels; he is a big-league connector and insisted we meet. Obviously, he had no idea what the exact outcome would be, but he definitely suspected something good would come of it. He was right. Both of our lives changed with that one introduction.

After graduating from Penn State in 2006, Ryan had taken the first job he could get: at a top pharmaceutical company in his home state of New Jersey, where there are as many pharma companies as there are strip malls. He sat down at a cubicle

xvi   INTRODUCTION

every day, collected a reasonable paycheck for a wet-behind-
the-ears college grad, but was . . . miserable.

He wasn't alone. His lifelong friend and freshman-year
roommate, Ryan Healy (people referred to them as "the
Ryans"), was sitting in a cubicle down in Washington, DC,
feeling equally demoralized by his first job. They complained to
each other often about how unhappy they were. Eventually, the
Ryans decided to do something about it.

They realized that if they were going to be in jobs that
were financially stable but soul deadening, they might as well
use that stability to "moonlight our own destinies," as Ryan
(Paugh) puts it.

Blogging was just becoming trendy, especially among
Gen X and baby-boomer recruiters, hiring managers, and HR
professionals who were just starting to add Generation Y and
millennials (like the Ryans) to their teams. But they were having difficulty working with this new breed of worker, and that
angst found its way onto their blogs. These young upstarts were
"Narcissistic." "Entitled." "Disloyal." Newspapers and magazine
articles—along with books like *Generation Me*—were dedi-
cated to lambasting the group. "But nobody from our generation was speaking up," says Ryan. The Ryans decided to create
a blog, Employee Evolution, to be that voice.

They blogged about the clash of generations in the workforce from their perspective, defended their peers, and at-
tempted to debunk the stereotypes associated with us. People
started to take notice. Both the *Wall Street Journal* and the *New
York Times* ran features on them; Morley Safer anchored a segment on *60 Minutes*.

And a funny thing happened: They discovered that they weren't alone in their dissatisfaction with the status quo of the working world. Nor were they the only ones who resented the generational stereotypes. They met with and supported a number of bloggers, many of whom became good friends, who shared their beliefs. One of whom was a woman named Penelope Trunk.

Trunk, a Gen Xer, had written a book called *Brazen Careerist: The New Rules for Success*, a career guide for Gen Y. It became so popular that it spawned a column in the *Boston Globe* and a controversial career blog that's still around today, but she was looking to do something bigger with the brand. That's where the Ryans came on the scene.

Trunk didn't know what she wanted to do next with her brand, but she knew she wanted it to be a startup and that she didn't want to do it alone. She found Employee Evolution through seeing them comment frequently on her blog (they were huge fans). She wanted the Ryans to be her partners in her next venture.

Together, they created Brazen Careerist 2.0: an online community for young professionals entering the workforce to share their challenges and frustrations and offer each other support. The bloggers they had befriended earlier, along with the ones they met through Employee Evolution, became their anchors (more about anchors later). In 2009 *Mashable* had dubbed their little startup "one of the top social networking destinations for Gen Y."

Flash-forward to 2010. The Ryans were now living in Madison, Wisconsin, where Trunk lived with her family (because when you're in your early twenties and your partner has two kids, a husband, and a home, you go where she tells you to). They had raised more than $1 million in funding, and they brought hundreds of thousands of people onto the Brazen Careerist platform. But they weren't making any money. As Ryan puts it, "We had to make a big change, or—as startup folk like to call it when you have to go back to the drawing board—a pivot."

They had to bring in new leadership. One of their lead investors and a seasoned CEO who believed in them stepped in. Brazen Careerist was beginning to take new shape as a software-as-a-service platform providing speed networking opportunities helping recruiters and job seekers, students and alumni at universities, and any other A-B combination you can think of connect online. It was a brazen move inspired by the phenomenon of Chat Roulette (yes, the one with all the creepy naked people).

And something unexpected: the company started making money! They brought on big-name clients, and the company was reborn as a SaaS technology play: Brazen Technologies.

As thrilled as Ryan was to see the company he cofounded start to see some success, he also started feeling like his time at Brazen was coming to an end. He was (and still is) a community builder at heart, and he felt like he couldn't contribute the best parts of himself to the team.

One afternoon he sat on a beach in Chatham, Massachusetts, with his friend Dan Schawbel. That's when his life changed. Schawbel suggested that he connect with an entrepreneur named Scott Gerber, who was working on something that was right up his alley. Scott had studied film at New York

University, and while he was still in college he became a very successful producer. He knew nothing about business—he relied on Google to help him decipher terms like *P&L*. His family couldn't help him; they weren't entrepreneurs or moguls. He had no formal mentors or advisers to counsel him on what he was doing right or wrong; he relied on instinct, salesmanship, wagonloads of naïveté, and . . . his Type A chutzpah.

He created a viable business and managed to make a lot of money his junior year—which he promptly lost a year later, largely because he was a rookie, made stupid mistakes, and had no network around him to help him deal with the business challenges he faced. At that moment he made himself a promise. He never wanted another entrepreneur to experience the same feelings of loneliness or lack of support that he had. He never wanted another young businessperson to go blindly without a network or any other connections, as he had. He vowed that if he ever found financial success, he would create a group where like-minded young entrepreneurs could help each other solve the types of challenges he faced.

After graduation in 2005—to the chagrin of his "real job" touting family—he took the last seven hundred dollars to his name and built another company, called Sizzle It!, which produced promotional videos (or "sizzle reels") for PR and marketing firms. He learned from past mistakes, and it did quite well. It generated substantial profits and had a who's who client roster of many of the world's largest brands and advertising agencies.

Two years later he made good on his promise, and the first iteration of the Young Entrepreneur Council, commonly known today as YEC, was born.

In 2010, after the recession hit, Scott began sharing his story with universities and youth entrepreneurship groups. He felt students could relate to him as a peer and find value and inspiration in his journey. After all, he was only a few years older than the students he was speaking to.

Then the media came a-knocking, which caught the attention of dozens of young entrepreneurs from around the country. The message resonated with them, and many would end up reaching out to him and joining him as he continued to speak with students and youth groups. As the press interest around youth entrepreneurship and the Young Entrepreneur Council hit fever pitch, Scott broadened the concept yet again. He began asking up-and-coming entrepreneurs from around the country to send him their business questions and challenges. He would then funnel them to his newly assembled group of successful entrepreneurs, who would answer those questions. He then partnered with several of the media outlets who had been covering his efforts, such as *Inc.* magazine, *Time*, and the *Wall Street Journal*, and published his group's collective responses in their publications.

As more questions and more press outlets wanted to take part, Scott continued reaching out to other successful entrepreneurs his age to join his group. They, in turn, introduced him to people in their networks. One of them was named . . . Dan Schawbel.

After a month's worth of back-and-forth, Ryan and Scott finally got on the phone. We clicked big-time. That's when things got serious. "I remember thinking, 'Wow, my business advice is being shared alongside advice from Alexis Ohanian, the cofounder of Reddit!'" Ryan recalls. "There had to be some-thing more we could do with this group." Ryan started flying into Manhattan from Madison regularly, and we'd walk around the city all day long, talking about building the next great en-trepreneurial organization. We ate more Panera Bread than we could handle but burned off the carbs just as quickly with every step we took while formulating our vision.

Together, we realized that it was possible to do both *good and well* at the same time. First and foremost, we wanted to help other people with their businesses. But we also wanted to be able to create enough value for ourselves to ensure that the Young Entrepreneur Council wouldn't become just another one of Startupland's failed meet-up groups due to lack of care and management. It wasn't easy. We both worried: Would people want what we offered in a formal manner? Would they be will-ing to pay for it?

The answer, we discovered, was *yes*.

We didn't realize how much value we'd been creating or how valuable we were to other people. (But more on that later.) Slowly, what began as an organic movement turned into a legitimate, sustainable business. Eventually, we both left the businesses we started to step into YEC full-time and grew it into the thriving organization that it is today.

By 2012 YEC had become a huge resource for entrepre-neurs and media alike. Today, YEC is composed of more than seventeen hundred entrepreneurs in North America forty years old and under, whose companies make more than $1 mil-lion annually in revenue. The group has led to thousands of meaningful business connections, and the business generates several million dollars in revenue annually. Our success with YEC even inspired the creation of other membership groups for professionals in different business sectors through partnerships with organizations like *Forbes* and *Men's Health*. These communities sit alongside YEC now in our new umbrella company, The Community Company, which works with media enterprises, global brands, and celebrities to build professional organizations that help our partners create greater engagement and customer affinity.

And we owe it all to an introduction made by a third party who connected two guys living in two separate parts of the country who shared very similar ideas and ideals. Thanks to our mutual friend Dan, who had the foresight to connect two guys—two connectors who think and act like connectors!—we were able to create something amazing. We took the ball Dan tossed our way and ran with it. We used our methodology to build social capital and, eventually, saw great financial success.

Let's be clear: none of this would have happened if not for a single connection from our dear friend Dan Schawbel, the Superconnector who saw an opportunity for two people with different strengths to create and make something magical happen.

"I had a gut feeling," Dan later told us. "In my head I'm thinking, 'The two personalities are very different, but they are in effect trying to do the same thing.'" His gut was right. If we hadn't teamed up, YEC would never have made the transition from a small idea to a movement and then led to a successful business. *That's* the power of a good connection—and the power of a Superconnector. Again, a whole lot of value can be created with just one single connection with the right context, purpose, and reasoning. If we didn't trust Dan or Dan's judgment, or if we had chosen not to listen to him, we might have never met. Or we might have met and not taken the relationship any further. But we both recognized that this was a connection worth diving into. As a result, we built a business that has changed both of our lives for the better.

But we weren't the only ones whose lives changed. Dan's access, reach, and clout increased exponentially as well. His cachet grew along with his opportunities: He increased his direct and indirect access to media outlets and other entrepreneurs in YEC who could help him in his professional endeavors. He benefited from YEC, just by association. That's the kind of serendipitous good karma that more often than not comes back to a Superconnector, because of their goodwill and thoughtfulness in connecting others.

CHAPTER 1

THE END OF "NETWORKING"

On the one hand, meeting people is easier today than ever before. Thanks to social media, Facebook, Twitter, and a never-ending number of new platforms arising daily, it's simple to reach out to just about anyone in the world. You virtually poke them, they poke back, and suddenly they're one of your five hundred BFFs. Awesome!

As it became easier to "connect" with other people, we forgot what "connection" really meant. We conflated the two. "Connect" and "connection" are not the same thing. Most people strive to connect and repeat instead of connection and repeat. They're interested in breadth over substance. We are the exact opposite. There's a big difference between the kind of connecting social media has taught us to do and the kind we want you to follow.

See, here's the reality: "Networking" as we know it, as we have been taught it, is dead. Or, at the very least, it's on life support with little chance for recovery. In fact, we'd like to abolish the word altogether and substitute *connecting* for *networking*.

Who killed it? Well, in a way, we all played a role. You, us, your aunt Helen, and just about anyone else vying to get ahead in the world. Our more-is-more, networking-for-networking's-sake approach to social media, conference attendance, and, yes, even daily human interaction has bastardized this once reliable pillar of business success into a mere mirage.

Why didn't anyone tell you that networking kicked the bucket? Because there are entire industries, software companies, and consultants generating billions of dollars annually by continuing to give credence to this outdated, gluttonous approach to "relationship building."

The MLM industry—that's multilevel marketing—is a perfect example. Hundreds of companies out there have told people they should simply meet, "monetize," and repeat. Never mind that these practices have destroyed lives, financial futures, and friendships. And we let them! Each one of us is at fault. Our lack of awareness and unwillingness to change our behaviors are what led us here. We just keep following the same stale, antiquated networking techniques because we're told they will work. Rather than learning something new, we default to our familiar habits. But they don't work!

An ever-growing number of gurus, conference organizers, and MLM hucksters are feeding us antiquated "tips," "tricks," and "hacks" about how to best go about building valuable "relationships" (by *their* definition, that's code for "sales prospects").

Except it doesn't build relationships. Not even a little bit.

So why do we let ourselves continue down this path of networking for networking's sake and gross overuse of social media? Because we're addicts.

About 5 to 10 percent of all Internet users are screen junkies. A December 2014 study in the journal *Cyberpsychology, Behavior, and Social Networking* found that 6 percent of the world's population is addicted to the Internet. With about 7 billion people on the planet, that's roughly 420 million people who experience a huge rush when they log on, similar to the way drug addicts and alcoholics feel when they get a fix.

So, we are, quite literally, hooked on this stuff.

Back in the good old days—say, the beginning of the twenty-first century—networking was pretty standard. You went to events, you handed out business cards, and you pressed a button on LinkedIn and boom! You were "connected." Mission accomplished.

Never mind that you rarely took the relationship offline. Sure, you and your new BFFs may have emailed on occasion or placed each other on one another's generic mailing lists, but the relationship didn't progress much beyond that. Still, you dutifully continued on this path, amassing contact after contact. You were told that this was the right thing to do: In order to climb the corporate ladder or build business success, you have to schmooze with as many people as possible. You never know when that one right person might come along who can help advance your career or take your business to the next rung.

On one level, this is correct—you *don't* know whom you might meet and how they might rock your universe. But there's a better way to find them besides trolling gigantic auditoriums at, say, Ye Olde Trade Show. Rather than hopping around like a moleskin pouch in search of a business card, you're better off asking yourself: Is this *really* the best use of my time? Is this the smartest way I can achieve the outcome I desire?

Let us help you out here: *No, it is not.* There's a much better way to build meaningful, mutually beneficial relationships that yield real results.

Indeed, somewhere along the line, we lost sight of the actual purpose of networking: to build a mutually beneficial relationship with another person and maintain that relationship for the long term.

Stylistically (and the core thinking of the MLM industry), the mantras and blog fodder differ from speech to clickbait-headline blog post, but in essence the typical pitch reads something like this: "If you focus on building fans and followers on social media, regularly share content using 'inbound marketing' techniques, and attend networking events, you will be able to amass a giant network from which to extract value—and win big at business." Never mind the time and care it takes to get to know the actual people you meet; you can just "growth hack" (yes, that's a real buzzword—or buzzverb) your way to Rolodex success!

It's exhausting just reading it.

Here's the truth: The number of contacts and followers you have online does not trump real relationships. Being virtually or offline "connected" is not in itself valuable. Social capital cannot be measured in likes and shares. Instead, you have to acquire social capital and build trust and meaningful relationships through the right conversations, actions, and value exchanges with the right people. (By value exchange, we mean information, education, mentorship, a resource, or a connection—literally, a place where value is exchanged.)

Instead of asking, "How do I solve this business challenge?" a Superconnector thinks, "Who do I know who can help me solve this business challenge or directly connect me with the right people?" A Superconnector knows how to use social capital to solve business challenges with the same ease that a sommelier knows which wine to order with your steamed lobster (FYI: a chardonnay or nice white burgundy). We have spent hundreds of hours thinking about this and have created a methodical, systematic way, which is exactly what we will teach you to do in this book.

Mind you, we are not telling you to eradicate every single one of your old habits. We don't want you to veto all conferences or never post on Facebook again. Conferences can be wonderful tools; we've met a lot of amazing people at them. But you do need to rethink every aspect of your attendance, including your purpose and participation. We're not suggesting you never use social media or attend events ever again, but we are saying it's important to be smarter and more strategic about the things you do.

You'll still be using the same tools and real estate you've always used; you'll just use them in different ways, for a different reason. Technology, for example, has enormous benefits. But technology should be used as a tool to engage, enhance, convene, and understand how to read people's motives, interests, and desires.

Rather than relying on it exclusively, we want to teach you the right way to use platforms. We are not about purging the tools that have driven new business relationships over the past decade, but instead committed to learning how to be more strategic and make the best use of your time when others are simply creating more noise. This new skill set is something you'll need in the professional world.

CHAPTER 2

HOW TO THINK LIKE A SUPERCONNECTOR, NOT A NETWORKER

Here's the thing. Since we first met in 2010, the world has gotten a billion times busier and noisier. There is so much social media, and there are so many conferences and so many opportunities for meeting, which is why being a Superconnector is more important than ever. As social media continues to proliferate in the business and entrepreneurial worlds and society is overwhelmed by the overabundance of noise versus signal—that is, important, meaningful information/connections/value exchanges/knowledge sharing—it's clear that the right access and social capital will exponentially increase in value. And that those who own these silos of walled-off access to that social capital will be exponentially more valuable in the eyes of others than those who don't.

Harnessing the power of the right connections will be ever more vital in the years to come. To be prepared for this new reality is to better understand the convergence of business and community, how a new way of thinking is required to successfully navigate existing real-world channels and online platforms, what skill sets are needed in order to thrive in the social-capital generation, and why it's time we abandon our gluttonous mentality of networking for networking's sake in favor of a more curated, thoughtfully crafted approach.

It's happening already. Decision makers and tastemakers who can actually move your business or career forward are leaving oversaturated "networking" channels in droves, looking to more curated, invitation-only experiences and communities where they can maximize their value and protect their time. How can you reach them and, better yet, join forces with them and see bigger wins?

And reach them you must. Because like it or not, those folks who adapt to our changing times and master this relationship-building philosophy will become uniquely positioned to build value for themselves and others and will join the ranks of a new, sought-after force of elite professionals.

We want to teach you to do what we do. Not necessarily to become a world leader or captain of industry, but to become the center of influence in whatever circle you want to be in. The goal is to get you to think, speak, act, and win like a connector.

A *Superconnector*.

Connectors don't see the world the same way the rest of the world does. We speak differently. We make an impression differently. We use technology differently. And we control our surroundings differently.

There is a big difference between "networking" and "connecting."

Let's look at entrepreneur and former Arena League football player Lewis Howes, who is also the author of the *New York Times* best seller *The School of Greatness: A Real-World Guide to Living Bigger, Loving Deeper, and Leaving a Legacy.* He is also the host of a highly successful podcast, *The School of Greatness.*

Howes refuses to network. He simply won't do it. "I just connect and add value," he says. "Networking is more transactional. It's more focused on getting a result for yourself as opposed to thinking of how can you be of service to the other person in front of you that you meet and genuinely have interest in their needs as opposed to your needs."

"Networking" has selfish implications: you want something out of someone else, so you go around making strategic connections. "I think about it as someone who's trying to build a web of relationships that serve a professional goal, and expand that web as efficiently as possible, and leverage it as efficiently as possible, which is why I feel a little dirty even defining it," says Wharton professor Adam Grant, the best-selling author of *Give and Take: Why Helping Others Drives Our Success.*

A connector isn't in it for anything above the pleasure he or she gets from introducing two people to each other who might benefit from knowing one another. "So it's not just, 'Hey, I think you two should meet because one of you can help the other,'" says Grant. "It's 'I think you two should meet because you share a common goal. It would be valuable to both of you to know each other.'"

Keith Ferrazzi looks at it similarly. "The words *networking* and *networker* can suggest a self-serving purpose: that you're in it to see what you can get out of others. That never works," he says. "A connector is reaching out to form an alliance with the other person, offering to be of service first and foremost. Networkers like to 'work the room' and collect cards, but those cards don't really mean much if the other person isn't willing to take your calls because all you did was schmooze and move on. If you're already making an ask before the other person has a chance to breathe, you might be a networking jerk."

Connecting is about finding out what the other person needs and how you can help. "It doesn't have to be a huge thing, just something that benefits the person you're connecting with," he says. "A successful connector knows there's more value in leaving an event with one new friend or acquaintance that you can develop a mutually beneficial relationship with than contact information for fifty people you didn't spend any time getting to know."

In order to begin to see the world through a different lens and hear it with a different ear and analyze it with a different brain, you need to rethink the way you interact with everyone and everything in the world around you. How do you do this? Superconnectors have many attributes, but above all else they must be in possession of one thing: self-awareness.

What Makes Me Tick?

Self-awareness is all about understanding your strengths and weaknesses, your thoughts and motivations, so you can live your best self. It means knowing what you're good at and what you are less than good at. Sometimes that means actually avoiding the things you're not good at rather than having to get better at them. It also allows you to understand how other people perceive you. And this is hugely important, both personally and professionally.

Scott can speak to this from personal experience. As a student at New York University, he was one of six students selected to meet with a high-level Hollywood development executive. Scott's intent was to ask insightful, thoughtful questions. He knew that he didn't know very much about the process of how executives determined whether to greenlight or distribute a film. His idea was to listen and learn.

Unfortunately, his plan was thwarted. As soon as they got into the room, another student whipped out the screenplay she'd written and began pitching the executive on why he should make it. The other students were horrified. The gall! So self-indulgent! She hijacked the conversation and made it all about her. The development executive was so taken aback that the rest of the meeting became useless.

Had she had a fraction of self-awareness, she would have known that her behavior was unacceptable and would never allow for a meaningful relationship or connection to stem from such a meeting. But she had no clue. After the meeting, Scott asked her if she knew what she had done.

"Yes," she replied. "I made an impression!"

She was right—she did make an impression. But not the kind she wanted to make. Her behavior was colossally *un*-self-aware. But she had no idea. She thought she had clinched a job in Hollywood.

This was the first time Scott had truly seen someone in action who entirely lacked self-awareness. It caused enormous damage with someone who could have been a game changer.

For Superconnectors, self-awareness is also important because it plays a big role in the way others perceive you. And like it or not, the world is built on first impressions. People's perceptions of you, how much they remember or pay attention to you, whether they're engaged by you, whether they'll have another conversation or even want another conversation with you, what they'll tell others about you, and why they may seek you out in the future are all based on their initial encounter with you.

Research backs this up. Amy Cuddy is a social psychologist at Harvard Business School and the author of the book *Presence*. She found that the strongest influences that we have on one another derive from a person's *perceived* warmth and competence (the operative word being *perceived*). Interestingly, it's warmth—not competence—that's more important when assessing another person. When we assess ourselves, however, we believe that *competence* is more important than warmth. Cuddy also found that "power posing"—say, putting your hands on your hips like Wonder Woman—and acting confidently convey perceptions of competence.

Obviously, being self-aware doesn't magically occur overnight. It's going to require you to understand the ways you shine and . . . the ways you suck. You have to know your pitfalls and shortcomings. (We're sure you don't have many, but we all have things we can work on.) By becoming cognizant of your limitations, you can begin to define your purpose or vision.

For example, most people can't talk about themselves in a very smart or interesting way. (By "smart" we mean the ability to understand and articulate goals and not just list their CV.) You don't want to be known for just anything—you want to be known for something you care about and what you want others to care about. (This is where "thesis" comes into play. More on that later.) You want to understand the real value you have to offer instead of the value you think you need to deliver.

Vanessa Van Edwards, an author and behavioral investigator, figures out what makes people tick in her behavioral research lab. So she knows a thing or two about human behavior. "Most people think Superconnectors are very good 'people people,'" she says. "But I think it's the opposite. The best Superconnectors know themselves. It's not about knowing others; it's about knowing where you thrive, how you connect, your favorite conversation starter. The people who have studied themselves are the best connectors."

She freely admits that she started her company because she is a Recovering Awkward Person. Nor was she especially self-aware. Growing up, she focused on academics. She was comfortable in a classroom, but outside of class? Not so much. When she was a junior in college, a professor told her to study people the way she would study math or science. "He told me to make flash cards," she says with a laugh. And so she did.

"I made flash cards of conversation starters and then took notes," she says. "In that process I was also figuring out myself. But I told myself, 'People are hard. You know yourself better than anyone. You have nineteen years of experience in who Vanessa is. Focus on you first.'"

When you're self-aware, you learn to play to your strengths and minimize or eliminate your weaknesses.

This takes practice, of course. Dan Schawbel, for example, knows himself really well. He is an introvert; big, noisy groups make him uncomfortable. He knew that he would have to compensate for his shortcomings. So he decided to hold small Friday-night dinners for a handful of people. "I started a millennial dinner club where I meet with people once a month," he says. "That plays to my strengths. With two hundred people, I am not working the room. It's getting to know yourself."

We advise people to take an inventory. As in make a list, check it more than twice, and write down your answers on a piece of paper. When you're forced to write it down, you're forced to be truthful with yourself.

This is for your eyes only (unless you want to share it with someone else), so we encourage you to be honest. By looking into yourself, you can determine what needs adjustment, what calls for just a little tweaking, and what works in your favor.

Do you understand the concept of personal space?
Do you exude confidence or arrogance?
Are you a listener or a talker?
Do your words carry weight or air?
Are you a good public speaker, or are you better online?
Are you comfortable walking up to a stranger and striking up a conversation, or would that give you a panic attack?
How do others really see you upon first contact?
What sorts of things are you really bad at when it comes to meeting with people?
Do you need help getting organized?

Are you a good decision maker?

Do you take time getting back to people?

Do you hate conversations that aren't about your interests or matters of importance to you?

Do you like small talk?

Are you naturally inquisitive or close-minded?

Have you ever changed your position on a deeply held belief?

Do you lie? If so, why? Is it because you want to feel self-important or because you feel like you need to keep up and fit in?

Finally, are you okay with what you've learned about yourself? Is there anything that bears correction?

So, now what?

We asked Darius Foroux that very question. Foroux, who is Dutch, studied marketing in college for about six years (the school system in the Netherlands is different from ours). "I was always an average kid," he says. "I didn't belong to the smartest people. I also wasn't part of the dumbest people."

After (finally) graduating, he wondered what he should do next. He realized that he didn't know much of anything. So he went back to get a master's in business administration, and that's where his interest in productivity began. Because during that period he was one productive dude. By the end of 2010—the same year he was writing his master's thesis—he and his father started a laundry technology company, creating software and automation for laundries that wash for hotels and hospitals.

"I figured out that the power of productivity and especially just knowing yourself, knowing what you're good at and knowing what you're bad at, basically determines the outcome of your life in terms of happiness, in terms of everything," he says.

During that period he also started researching everything that he writes about today on his blog, dariusforoux.com /selfawareness. And over the past seven years he has only gotten deeper into personal development and productivity. "Productivity yields results—and results determine the outcome of your life," he says.

The company was successful, but he decided he wanted some experience at a corporation, so in 2014 he got a job at Gartner, an IT research company, and worked in London for about a year and a half. He was miserable. Working for a corporation just wasn't his thing. His direct, open style of communication clashed with the culture. He didn't feel that he was making a difference. He wasn't happy or proud.

So what happened? He thought of Aristotle, as one does, who noted, "Knowing yourself is the beginning of all wisdom." He took a step back and quit his job. He was going to focus on his strengths again, on entrepreneurship. "That's when I really developed true self-awareness," he says. "You hear [the term] pretty often, but how self-aware are you actually? The only way to answer that question for yourself is to look at your decisions." For example, do you base your decisions on your strengths, or do you just make decisions because everyone else is doing something?

Foroux often asks himself what he's good at and what he's bad at. "If you don't take the time to think about knowing yourself and having self-awareness and developing that, then almost everything you do is just almost like gambling, right?" he says. "You just take opportunities. You make decisions. You do things without really thinking about them. And then you have to wait and see whether it makes you happy."

We've done this ourselves, by the way. And what we learned has helped us immensely in our own lives.

Scott, for example, often makes business decisions in the moment, but sometimes that has been a negative in his business and connector life. Earlier in his career, acting quickly on introducing people backfired. He skipped critical thinking steps that could have avoided burning bridges or turning people off. While he still makes business decisions daily, he rarely acts impulsively anymore.

Ryan is a better listener than talker in group situations. This can be a strength and also a weakness, especially when more outgoing people are involved in a group conversation and his instinct is to take the backseat and let them tell their stories. "It's great to be a good listener, but difficult for me to make an impression and drive the conversation in these situations," he says.

To compensate, he often carves out one-on-one time with the people who matter to him. Sharing a cup of coffee at a cozy café is probably more valuable than an open bar at a group networking event.

CHAPTER 3

WHAT TYPE OF CONNECTOR ARE YOU?

Erica Dhawan is an expert on collaboration who advises many leading brands and global organizations. She has degrees from MIT, Harvard, and Wharton. When she speaks, most people tend to listen. We certainly do. Dhawan, the coauthor of *Get Big Things Done: The Power of Connectional Intelligence*, realized that not only are people introverts and extroverts, but they also have different ways of connecting with other people. According to Dhawan, there are three types of connectors:

Thinkers
Enablers
Connection executors

Thinkers are curious to the max. They have a hundred ideas a minute; they're just not always the best at executing them.

Enablers can assemble people together and share ideas with them. Enablers love to introduce people to one another.

Connection executors are the accomplishers. They take other people's ideas and make them happen.

"You can have a lot of Enablers coordinating, but if they're not bringing new ideas to the table, it doesn't get done effectively," she says. "Or we'll go to a company and find that 90 percent of their executive team are Thinkers. They're trying to launch more tech-savvy innovation, and they realize that no one is going to do it! So one of the first things we do is help people really understand what are the collaboration styles, what are the gaps and strengths, and how they design teams to more effectively leverage these styles."

It's important to determine what type of connector you are so that you can figure out your strengths and weaknesses. If you don't understand your type, how are you supposed to find others who can help fill in the gaps where you have weaknesses? How do you know where to focus your energy? "It gives a sense of the type of person you should partner with and making sure that they are someone who connects differently from them," says Dhawan. This is something we did instinctively: since Ryan is an introvert and Scott is an extrovert, we complement each other.

The reason we like to reference Erica's work is because determining what type of connector you are is a great way to develop a stronger sense of self-awareness. You can home in on strategies that will work for you as a connector and avoid them, or find partners to fill in the gaps in all of the areas in which you're weak. You don't have to think of it as gospel, either. Remember, Superconnectors are great at learning from the people around them (as we are from our friend Erica!), while at the same time making their own rules.

If we were to categorize ourselves, Scott would be a Thinker. He loves big ideas and has never been accused of not having a strong-enough opinion. Ryan, on the other hand, is a really great executer, which is why he naturally fit into the role of chief operating officer (COO) at The Community Company. But our strengths intersect as Enablers, which we can offer to our company and the organizations we have created in a very symbiotic way.

Emotional Intelligence

Now that you're self-aware and have figured out what kind of connector you are, it's time to explore your emotional intelligence.

You may have heard something about "emotional intelligence," or EI. The concept was coined by researchers Peter Salovey and John D. Mayer, who describe it as "the subset of social intelligence that involves the ability to monitor one's own and others' feelings and emotions, to discriminate among them and to use this information to guide one's thinking and actions." It was later made popular by psychologist Daniel Goleman, who published a best-selling book, *Emotional Intelligence*, in 1995. Goleman argued that IQ shouldn't be the sole measure of a person's abilities; rather, their emotional awareness and intelligence also count. A lot.

Goleman defines EI as "the capacity for recognizing our own feelings and those of others for motivating ourselves, and for managing emotions well in ourselves and in our relationships." EI is more about how you care about other people; empathy is one of its core tenets. "Everyone has a deep desire to be understood, to have their human needs being taken care," says Jayson Gaignard, the founder of MastermindTalks, an invitation-only event for entrepreneurs.

Gaignard likens empathy to something the best marketers in the world can achieve. Terrible marketers are those who will talk about the product, about things that are inconsequential to the buyer. But the best marketers think and message with purpose. "I always say that great marketers have the unique ability of putting themselves in the shoes of their prospects," he says, "understanding their wants, needs, desires, and fears often better than they do. To be great at relationships, you need to do the same."

Scott has personally experienced this sort of generosity. Not long after meeting a man named John Ruhlin for the first time, Scott was heading to a three-day business trip to Nowhere, Michigan. Ruhlin is the cofounder and CEO of the Ruhlin Group and the author of *Giftology*; he and his team have created gift packages for some of the largest companies and pro sports teams in the world. Anything you want to know about gift giving—he's your guy.

Scott's iPhone had crashed two weeks earlier, and the repair company had tried—and failed—to fix it three times. Now, Scott is tethered to his phone; he is on his phone for business twelve to fifteen hours a day, via email, phone, Slack, or other apps. It was worse than losing an arm or a leg. "It was disabling and causing me stress like you wouldn't believe," says Scott. "This isn't just a phone to me; it's my gateway to my entire business and network."

The phone repair company had given him a temporary phone: an iPhone 4, which wasn't able to run a single app. The battery drained in one hour.

When Ruhlin met him, Scott was a head case. "I was at the end of my rope because the company fixing my phone just told me it might be another two weeks before I got my phone back right after I had shipped it, when they originally told me three days," he says.

But guess what? Ruhlin to the rescue! Fifteen hours later, when Scott opened the door to his hotel room in the Upper Peninsula of Michigan (with a now dead iPhone 4 to boot), there, along with a bottle of champagne and a handwritten note, was a brand-new iPhone 6 Plus, a personalized phone that was ready to be used immediately. Ruhlin—whom Scott had met only once before!—had found out Scott's phone carrier and the hotel he was staying in from his assistant and overnighted him a loaner, to be used until his own arrived. No fees. No surcharges. No deadline to return it. Scott couldn't believe it. "It shows he was not only listening to me," Scott recalls, "but understood a major pain point. I was like, 'This is impressive and so incredibly thoughtful. I'm never going to forget this.'" And he hasn't.

Ruhlin shrugs it off. "It's fun for me to see what I can pull off and do," he says. "It's semiaddictive. It's fun when I can pull off the impossible." It was also emotionally intelligent.

But you can't fake EI! As Jayson Gaignard puts it, "There are people who care and then people who *genuinely* care. The latter can't be faked," he says. "You can't fake empathy or caring; you have to truly care about what you do. If you don't, you have to be honest and not pursue this type of relationship building."

Picking Your Pond

It's not enough to be emotionally intelligent, though. You want to be aware of all the things that make you tick, including the sort of place you're comfortable inhabiting.

Most people think you need to live in New York, LA, or San Francisco with the titans of industry to build life-altering relationships. Wrong! You don't need to live in dense populations where you can meet a lot of people. The most self-aware and successful Superconnectors root themselves in the places where they feel happiest and most stable. This is fundamental to having a satisfying life, but also a necessity if you want to build relationships with meaning and depth.

A few years ago, Van Edwards moved from Los Angeles to Portland, Oregon. It was necessary: bigger cities make her anxious. She knew that she couldn't thrive as a Superconnector in a spread-out, impersonal place like LA. So she left.

At first it was scary; she knew only one person in Portland. "I thought, 'I'll have no network,'" she recalls. She was wrong. In fact, her entire perspective on and approach to meeting people changed once she moved from a big pond to a small pond. Within a few months, it was bigger than her network in LA— the city where she grew up!

As a human behavior hacker, Van Edwards wanted to run a test—could she, from scratch, grow her network to be bigger than her network in Los Angeles? She realized that for her, it was way better to be a big fish in a small pond. "I believe everyone has situations where they thrive and survive, and the key to strong networking is never putting yourself in survival situations," she says. "If you hate loud bars, don't put yourself in a situation like that."

Beyond that, the self-described "science geek" cites something called the Similarity Attraction Effect: the idea that people like to surround themselves with people like them. "Opposites attract is a cliché not based in science," she says. "Every time you have a mutuality, a commonality, you will attract each other."

What this means is that if you are in a small pond, you're much more aware of that pond. Whereas people in Los Angeles may be somewhat (if not more) ambivalent about the place, "in Portland, they are *Oregonians*," she says, enunciating each syllable for emphasis. "So in every pond, you find a similarity."

The cool thing is that all of us can fit into multiple ponds. We might not think of it that way, but we all have a host of arenas. Van Edwards, for example, is an entrepreneur. She is female. She is a social psychology expert. Right there are three groups she could join. And she did. As it happens, there was also a group in Portland for women entrepreneurs in technology. She hooked up with it, too. "The right pond is the one where you are fascinated by everything in it," she says.

Ryan is very much the same way. The minute he arrives at New York's Penn Station and hits Seventh Avenue, the first thought to pop into his head is "When can I go home?" He's just not a big-city guy.

When he and Scott first got serious building YEC, he knew that he wanted to move back east from Wisconsin. New York would have been a smart place to hang his hat: Scott was there (he, not surprisingly, thrives as a Superconnector in big cities). But Ryan knew he wouldn't have the sense of stability and comfort he needed to let his own relationship-building prowess soar. Instead of moving to Manhattan, he chose . . . Boston, a much smaller city, where the entrepreneurial community felt more intimate and easy to navigate.

Where you ultimately live determines how well you build strong relationships that will propel you forward in life. But if you're living in a place that gives you the hives, then you won't be successful (or happy). If you're the kind of person who gets an adrenaline boost from a bustling metropolis like Manhattan, then that's where you should go. If you find comfort in a smaller city, then that's the place for you. We know Superconnectors who live on rural farms in the Midwest because that's where they're the happiest. Anyone, anywhere, can be a Superconnector. Who you are is ultimately more important than where you live.

Curiosity

Curiosity is the engine that informs, leads, and inspires conversations. Superconnectors are extremely curious individuals. They care about learning, expanding their horizons, and getting as much information as they can from others in order to be helpful later on. They ask bucketloads of questions. If you're

not a naturally curious person and you're not naturally inquisitive, well, now's a good time to try to change that. It's really
not that difficult—it's not like we're asking you to magically
grow five inches. We're just asking you to be curious about the
people you are talking to, to ask some questions, and to shut up
and listen.

"Listening is probably the most critical trait for anyone who
wants to become a Superconnector, since you're the one reaching out to the potential connection," says Keith Ferrazzi. "Curiosity about someone other than yourself is also important."

Okay, fine. But what if you truly are not interested in how
the world works? (Hard to imagine, we know, but some people
really aren't.) Can you develop curiosity? In his book *Curious:
The Desire to Know and Why Your Future Depends on It*, author
Ian Leslie offers an array of tips on how to become curious.
Suggestions include going to a real-life bookstore or library
(there are some left, thankfully) and getting lost in the shelves,
reading everything you can get your hands on on a wide swath
of subjects, and not solely relying on Google for information.

Final thought: If you're not a naturally curious person, fear
not. If you can train yourself to ask a lot of questions, you won't
be at a disadvantage.

We will go into deep detail in Chapter 8 about what makes
a good question (as well as what questions really suck), but
what's important to note here is that a curious person doesn't
usually accept the first response to a question as *the* answer.
Instead, they just see it as the outer layer.

Good questions have answers that are like layers of an
onion—you can continue to peel them away. The deeper you

go with follow-up questions leads to layers with more depth and value than the layers before.

For example, you might be satisfied by the simple exospheric answer to the question "What do you do?" (e.g., I'm project manager for XYZ Company). If that's the case, your curiosity levels might need some help. The deeper, more meaningful nuggets of information lie in layers beneath that you can access by asking follow-up questions. For instance:

"What do you like the most about your job?"
"What's one exciting thing you're working on right now?"
"What challenges about your work are keeping you up at night?"
"What types of opportunities are you looking for beyond what you're currently doing?"

Moving past the basics and into an area with more depth and substance is what separates a simple networker from someone with Superconnector potential. Remember this the next time you're meeting someone new. Dig a little deeper and flex your curiosity muscles.

CHAPTER 4

THE ART OF SELECTIVITY

People notice the company you keep. For better or for worse, whom we surround ourselves with is a reflection of who we are. So you want to make sure that you surround yourself with folks you admire and respect, who can set the tone for the whole foundation. You don't just haphazardly build a network with anyone who will communicate with you. You want to find people who'll have influence over the group. People who believe what you believe and buy into your thesis. People who are already connected in the circles that are meaningful to them.

Superconnectors are selective in everything they do: the time they manage, the company they keep, the people they put around them. It doesn't mean you are a snob and that you think you are better than everyone else. It just means you're cognizant of your time.

We are all busy; we're all trying to manage our time effectively. While you could give your time to fifty people, you would most likely make less of an impact than if you focused your energy on five people, especially five people who can become your zealots and take your mission to another five people, and so on and so forth.

Superconnectors are some of the most focused people we know. They hone their actions keenly.

Darrah Brustein founded Network Under 40 after a friend who had recently finished college and was working at an international law firm in Atlanta, where Brustein was living, complained that all of her friends had scattered around the country. She didn't really have a social circle anymore, and she didn't know what to do about it. Brustein racked her brain, trying to think of events where her friend could meet genuine people. She couldn't think of anything. So she did it herself.

The first event was "electric," with ninety-four people, ninety of whom were friends of Brustein's. So she continued throwing these events, and they grew into hundreds of attendees each month and soon got national press. People requested she throw similar events in their cities. So she did.

Brustein is well aware that you can add meaningful value to only a select group of people before the frequency with which you're able to provide value diminishes. "You can't develop relationships or help other people develop them if you're not who you really are," she says. "You need to be able to present an authentic version of yourself, and the right people will resonate with it and gravitate toward you."

That does not mean you have to get along with everyone or become everyone's best friend. "You can statistically have only X number of relationships, like 5 close ones, 50 secondary ones, and about 150 tertiary ones, and then everyone else falls into a big old pool," she says.

So she often does a little relationship housekeeping. "It's important to consider the five people who are in your inner circle, because they are going to deeply and profoundly influence you," she says. "It's important to know that the way people view you from the outside is going to have a lot to do with the people with whom you're surrounding yourself. So be sure not only that they're life-giving for you but also that they help you to be a bigger and better version of yourself simply because they're motivating just based on who they are. But remember too that people are going to draw snap and instant judgments of you based on this circle, so make sure that you're selecting wisely."

Your intention doesn't have to be anything radical, by the way.

In 2006 Elliott Bisnow was a twenty-year-old college student at the University of Wisconsin, with no mentor and no network. And he wanted them desperately. So he found twenty young entrepreneurs who were doing really cool things and called them out of the blue. He invited them on an all-expenses-paid ski trip to Alta, Utah, which his mother helped him plan. All of these people were up-and-comers: Josh Abramson and Ricky Van Veen had not yet founded CollegeHumor; Blake Mycoskie had not yet turned Tom's Shoes into an empire. All Bisnow knew was that they were people he wanted to know.

Before Bisnow's first ski trip, he had one goal: to get twenty interesting, kind, good people together, "with the intention of getting half a dozen great new relationships out of it."

He got that, and then some. Those original people invited people on the second trip, who then invited people for the third trip, and so on. The community kept getting bigger: today, there are thousands of people in what he called the "Summit Series" (now just Summit).

Admittedly, the idea of "curating" people the way you would some artifact in the Louvre sounds kind of obnoxious. On the other hand, you have to think about the sorts of people you want to surround yourself with. There is power in association.

Bisnow defines it as "lifestyle design," that is, giving thought to whom you're going to spend time with. "Are you going to create a life where you eat fast food and work later hours and your family comes second, where you have characters in your life who are not a good influence? Or are you going to surround yourself where health and wellness happen every day and the people around you care about the world and planet? It's picking your friends and where you live and what you eat and how you live *intentionally*."

Incidentally, *exclusivity* has never been a word he has used. He prefers *self-selecting*. "We are just trying to get people who are really kind and passionate about the world together," he says. "I don't think that criterion is exclusive. Any person can self-select into it."

To some people, selectivity means being exclusive in the form of a structured, formal group. To others, it could be the company you keep. You don't have to be everybody's best friend.

So how do you separate those you want to invest in from those you don't? Mitch Kanner, the founder and CEO of 2

Degrees, a company that connects brands with people of influence to create cultural moments, agrees. Kanner has been credited with discovering the opportunity, connecting the parties, and causing the release of Jay-Z's *Magna Carta Holy Grail* album with 1 million Samsung phone owners; he was once named to *Advertising Age*'s list of "Hottest Rolodexes," but he's totally under the radar. He isn't interested in notoriety. He's interested in results. "Nurture those people whom you are able to execute unique, strategic, big ideas with and in success develop long-term trusted relationships with, because real relationships last," Kanner notes. "From a business perspective, those same people grow and evolve and continue to collaborate with you. It's all about trust and famous ideas that work."

Kanner prides himself on working with a select cadre of significant clients rather than a large, impersonal group. He mostly operates on principles that include talent, personality, ability to execute, partnership, and intelligence. Does he have anything in common with them as people? Are they good people?

And no matter what, never, ever compromise your values—even if it puts you in a potentially negative situation with someone.

That is: You are creating your own world around you. You get to decide how people should interact with each other. You decide the rules of engagement. And that, in turn, determines how you build your community. You get to decide with whom you spend your precious time, building hands-on, deep relationships. But don't overextend yourself by trying to connect with too many people and doing too many things at once! This is a mistake many would-be Superconnectors make. By keeping that inner circle small, you'll be surprised how much more good you'll be able to do for the larger community of people in the world who care about the same things that you do.

Obviously, not everyone has a mountain at their disposal to help curate an elite community that makes for a Superconnector's fantasy. Let these stories of people like Bisnow and others inspire you, but please don't hold yourself to the same standards. Start curating and leveraging the art of selectivity in your own world with a simple assessment . . .

First, assess yourself. Ask: Am I in control of the relationships I have in my life, or am I giving that control to others? If the latter, how can I take the power back? And, more important, how will I use that power once I have it back in my possession?

This starts by determining what selectivity should look like in your life. Who is deserving of your time and why? Equally as important, who's not?

If I don't control most or all of my time, why do I feel the need to follow the lead of others?

Can I take that power back immediately or slowly? Why or why not?

If something is stopping me from controlling my own time, can I put a plan in place to lessen my time investment until I fully withdraw from such a person, commitment, or activity?

Next, assess your habits and activities. What activities did I take part in over the past week? What was worth my time? What wasn't? What would I definitely do again or invest more time in? What would I cut entirely?

Finally, assess others. Who did you spend your time with over the past week? Who was worth your time? Who wasn't?

Based on the people you've met with this past week, what types of people do you definitely want to invest more of your time in? What types of people do you want to cut entirely?

For each of these exercises, you can create a simple two-column chart. In one column, write down your traits and the traits of the people and activities you enjoyed investing time in (e.g., "Ambitious," "In my industry," "Valuable insights," and the like).

In the other column, write down your traits and the traits of the people and activities you didn't enjoy investing time in (e.g., "Not in my industry," "Wanted to watch movies all night," and so on).

This will help you weed out the people you don't want and focus more on the ones you do.

What's Your Authentically Authentic Thesis?

Your thesis is what you stand for, who you are, and what you believe in. Ideally, you should be able to utter all this in two sentences. Knowing this will help you define your goals.

You want to understand why you do the things you do. What do you care about, and why do you care about the things you care about? What do you want to be known for?

Not only can't the majority of people talk about themselves in a smart and interesting fashion, but they aren't sure what they're trying to accomplish in their work lives, either. They read a business book that tells them to do content marketing and create a personal brand in XYZ subject area, so they do it (or hire someone else to do it) and expect the world to come to them.

This is ass-backward. What's more, people know when you are being insincere. They can smell it from a hundred miles away. They know when you are doing something that doesn't come from a genuine place.

Indeed, there's a huge difference between strategically deciding, "I'm going to be authentic!" and having someone else say, "Now, *that* is one authentic person." Your goal should be not to promote your own authenticity but to pass other people's authentic-ometer. You want external authenticity and internal authenticity. You want to be authentically authentic!

Steve Sims, fifty, is the CEO of The Bluefish, the "world's most successful concierge," in his words. As he puts it, "I'm the guy who gets stuff done."

In his opinion, "'Authenticity' is a new fucking T-shirt! *Networking* has become the dirtiest word in business. You have to come to people with rawness—with what your message is."

People can tell if you are genuine, just from your intent and tone of voice. If you're off-putting and just doing the bare minimum, it's obvious. You know when you're having a real conversation instead of a superficial one, right?

If you recall, part of the reason we linked up is because we both wanted to help young entrepreneurs like us. We both wanted to help them get access to better people and resources. And thus, YEC was born. We are convinced that entrepreneurs came knocking because our thesis resonated in everything we wrote, tweeted, and posted, as well as how we spent our free time volunteering. We had clear values we wanted to espouse.

Virtues. We didn't just write about them or talk about them with the press; we lived them. We cared deeply about what we were talking about.

The point, though, is that our expertise grew from an organic place. We didn't start out focusing on keywords and taglines to get better search-engine optimization. It happened naturally, genuinely, growing from years of patience and consistency, because those who are transactional and sporadic will lose in the end. We practiced what we preached. We were hands-on and mentored other people. We launched a campaign to push a bill through Congress that would help ease youth unemployment and rallied other entrepreneurs, thought leaders, and politicians to get behind it. We even tried to get Stephen Colbert to give it the "Colbert Bump," a national campaign that received tremendous support from our audience. (It didn't work, alas, but we have hope that he's reading about it here and will come to his senses.)

But while we (humbly) acknowledge that we're good at what we do, we don't believe that a brazen attitude alone made us who we are today. It was the work we put in and our genuine care for that work. We didn't just talk a good talk; we backed it up with real action. If neither one of us cared about young entrepreneurs or Gen Y, whatever we wrote or said would have come off as empty, hollow, and insincere. People would have seen right through us, and they would have been right.

The moral of the story? Don't try to be something you're not.

That was something Allison Esposito, the founder of Tech Ladies, which connects women with the best jobs in tech, kept

in mind when she was building her community. Esposito recognized that women in technology needed a safe space. Her
idea was to "scale kindness." She had experienced sexual ha-
rassment and gender discrimination during her career. She
wondered, "How can we build solutions and use networking
and the power of a group of people to make the experience of
working in tech as a woman better?"

As Tech Ladies started growing, she started to feel a sense
of security that she'd never had in her career. "I thought, 'You
know . . . if something really bad happens that's out of my control, I have a couple of hundred people right now that I could
talk to and network with and lean on for my next job," she says.
"That started to feel like the first job security I'd had in my career, and that's what really drew me in." Today, Tech Ladies has
fifteen thousand members.

With a well-crafted purpose, you can define which relationships matter most for you to cultivate, learn how to create
the foundation for those relationships, and decide how you will
maintain them over time.

CHAPTER 5

THE POWER OF ASSOCIATION

Superconnectors know what questions to ask. They also tend to be great listeners. But they sometimes like to have someone by their side, another person to bounce things off of. We call them our anchors. But for now it might be helpful to think of them as a *connector*'s connector.

A large part of what made YEC so valuable was that from early on, we had compiled a small group of people who understood our mission: to create a small sphere of people willing to let their guard down and share and support one another in a professional capacity. When we opened it up and grew that community through referrals, it took on a life of its own. Members we helped with connections or visibility in the press would naturally tell their entrepreneurial peers and so on.

We called those people our "anchors," and they are basically trusted advisers and the foundation on which any successful community is built. The bedrock. Long-term connections who will always be there for you.

Anchors are so important because they're your gateway to meet other amazing people and set the stage for what others will think of you. An anchor can be anyone from a group organizer (whether for-profit or nonprofit) to an adviser to a friend or family member. It doesn't matter who they are; more important is that they're the cornerstone of whatever it is you want to do. They have both short-term potential (introducing you to people, offering you association to further progress your relationship building) and long-term potential (exponentially building out and maintaining your network with your remaining at the center).

When we first started YEC, for example, we only had about thirty members. The idea was to build the foundation and grow it from there. If you can create something special that people care about—if, say, you have five or ten real estate investors who are amassing high-level information from each other—that's infinitely more valuable than putting them in touch with eight thousand people.

It's important to assemble people who you believe are going to buy into what you're going to do for the collective. You also want to provide constant and consistent training so that they're able to run with the torch themselves once the comfort level has been achieved.

Why? Because you cannot scale you! You can't be everywhere at once. So you want people—ambassadors—who will be able to do this themselves, so they feel ownership.

Superconnectors associate with these anchors to fill in the gaps between their weaknesses and strengths, as well as for credibility and the value of association. Your anchors help you demonstrate to others the company you keep. They also enable you to meet other people more fluidly from other people's networks. If you're introverted, this might mean you'd work with an extrovert to pull you out of your shell. If you're extroverted, it might mean being with someone who helps bring you back down to earth and connect you with introverts you want to meet who might otherwise be shaken by your superoutgoing personality type.

An anchor gives credibility and value and shows that by association, the person is legit. It's the idea that when you get into a circle of the most powerful people on earth, if you're being brought in by an insider who already has a track record, trust, and relationships, you have instant credibility. Doesn't matter if it's a major circle or a small, intimate gathering of local professionals.

Over the years, we have each met amazing people because we act as each other's anchors. Sure, Scott, the ultimate extrovert, has introduced people to Ryan. But Ryan has also introduced people to Scott—specifically, other introverts who are valuable to know, who may have been intimidated to meet Scott and would have shied away from the more traditional places where Scott meets people (like any large social gathering). The fact that Ryan knows them instantly gives Scott credibility. And vice versa. But anchors aren't only personality driven. An anchor could also simply be someone who can pull you into their world to break the ice.

Incidentally, Jayson Gaignard, of MastermindTalks, did not start out as a Superconnector. His goal was to gather people together for a remarkable experience with huge social influence. He trusted his network to do its job and introduce only the people who are meaningful to him. "I believe you can get credibility through association," he says.

Gaignard came to his new vocation in a rather interesting way. In August 2011, he attended an event called "Opening the Kimono," run by best-selling author Tim Ferriss, of *4-Hour Workweek* fame. It was geared toward authors and cost ten thousand dollars a pop. Was it worth it to spend ten thousand dollars? Actually, yes. Gaignard was surrounded by brilliant thinkers and businesspeople, and he got a chance to meet Ferriss in person. "It opened my eyes to the value of the idea that if you're the smartest person in the room, you're in the wrong room," he says. "I was definitely in over my head."

He invited Ferriss to come speak in Canada in May 2013, which became the very first MastermindTalk. Gaignard could not pay speakers, but he already had Ferriss on deck, and people wanted in. Through that association, he landed other well-known names, such as authors and entrepreneurs Ryan Holiday and Lewis Howes. Five other people whom he'd also met at the 2011 "Kimono" event also signed on. "Going into that first event, I had no credibility, but having the credibility of Tim and Ryan rubbed off on me," Gaignard says.

You might be surprised who your wingmen and wingwomen turn out to be.

The Pyramid of Influence

We've been told that the highest-paid executives or the ones with the most press recognition are the key people to meet. But if you ask most of them whom they trust, you probably wouldn't know any of the people they mention. Most of *their* influencers are under the radar.

Superconnectors understand who the right people to connect with are: those who impact other people's decisions and ideas. We think of it as a Pyramid of Influence.

At the top of the pyramid is the person you want to reach. Most people's instinct is to zip right up the pyramid and reach out directly to that person. Why waste time with anyone else? Ah, but here's the thing: in order to reach him or her, you want to go *lower* on the pyramid. Those are the people who are the Influencers, the ones who have unfettered access to the person in charge. That could be their spouse. Or assistant.

Imagine you want to meet Richard Branson. It's unlikely that he's going to be interested in meeting you. Not because you're lame, but because he gets so many requests. Rather than going right to him, you should go to someone lower on the totem pole.

Keith Ferrazzi acknowledged this issue in a widely read blog post, "How I Avoided the Receiving Line and Met Hillary Clinton," which was published on LinkedIn on May 1, 2015. At the time of their meeting, way back in the 1990s, Clinton was first lady and Ferrazzi was the chief marketing officer (CMO) of Starwood Hotels. He had gone to an event where she was the keynote speaker; afterward, the place was jammed with people set on meeting her.

While the masses were clamoring for Hillary's attention, Ferrazzi noticed a woman standing off to the side. Every so often, she spoke directly to Hillary. *Aha!* She was not some random woman whispering into the first lady's ear—she was Clinton's executive assistant, whom he calls "Kelly." Ferrazzi started chatting her up, finding out about her life and her family. When he learned she was taking a vacation, he offered her a free upgrade for her accommodations.

"From an early age, I've keenly understood the criticality of maintaining warm relationships with those who manage the lives of important people, so we stayed in touch," he says. "I'd reach out to Kelly regularly, offering whatever value I could, and I'd never ask for favors from her boss since my friendship at that time wasn't with the first lady—it was with the woman who controlled much of her schedule and time."

When Clinton and Kelly came through Southern California, where Ferrazzi lived, he offered to make introductions that the team might want or need during their time off (which, of course, they did not have). Finally, thanks to his "relational capital with her office," Ferrazzi was invited to an exclusive event where he finally got the chance to meet Hillary face-to-face. He made such an impression on her that he was invited to the White House for the Clintons' last Christmas in office. When he ran into her years later at the Clinton Global Initiative, she remembered him well enough to ask about his kids.

The moral of the story is this: "When developing relationships, it's always best to look not just at the people you want to know but at those around them. Their staff aren't just 'gatekeepers'; often, they are lifeline relationships as well," he says.

"When you're of service to their confidants, and generous to them, you're being of service to them. Thought leaders, business leaders, major politicians—all need strong, loyal staff members to keep them up-to-date and on track. Any help you provide is noticed and ripples out. The key is to be patient and to understand that the more you establish yourself as an ally and a friend to your contact's staff, the more you'll be seen as a crucial member of a team and part of that person's inner circle," he says.

Now, you may not be in a position to meet the first lady. But the principle still applies to other people. Let's take it down a few notches.

In a small town, who is the person who's got his fingers on the pulse of almost everything? That's usually someone in a professional service position, like a lawyer, accountant, or someone who serves group organizers or nonprofits in a business capacity. There are many, and most are highly qualified. However, the most successful attorneys and professionals are also very well connected. It's also easier to get their attention when you're first starting out.

Say you are a top-tier attorney. Your key to success is to be highly connected to the business community in town. You constantly need to meet people; by default, if you are the most reputable in town and seen as the best at what you do, then you are a connector.

That said, you shouldn't just go and meet every accountant you can—but there are a select few who truly have access in almost every business ecosystem.

Ryan lives in Quincy, Massachusetts, a suburban city right outside of Boston. This is where he is raising his family; he plans on staying there for a long time. He cares a lot about seeing the town prosper and thinks that the current government isn't getting the job done fast enough. He's been looking for ways to get involved and support the town he is so invested in.

So where did he start? With a trip to the mayor's office—"by looking for groups of people who felt the same way that I did about making change in Quincy," he says.

His first connection was a lawyer he was sitting next to at a bar in downtown Boston. They struck up a conversation.

"Where do you live?" Ryan asked.

"Quincy," she replied.

"Hey, me too. Do you like living there?"

"Not bad, but I feel like they need to catch up with the rest of Boston," she said. "I'm working with some people to help push some changes."

Boom. He found his in. He was invited to attend a fundraiser for a new candidate for mayor and started finding new ways in which he could get involved and support the changes he wanted to see in his community.

There is no magic here—just a little strategy.

In this case, Google is your best friend. In a LinkedIn culture, you can find out just about anything you need to know about a person that's not confidential or private (and you might even learn that, too). It's the first place we go to see who is connected to whom and to do research on someone. Who knows? Maybe you have commonalities.

The Gift That Keeps on Giving

Ruhlin wasn't always a gifting guru. It came to him organically. He was in college studying to be a doctor and interned at Cutco, a cutlery, kitchen knives, and accessories company, to learn sales.

One day he noticed that Paul, the father of a girl he was dating, sent clients an extraordinary number of knives. But he didn't send them just to clients—he also sent knives to their spouses and business associates. "I was like, 'You're gonna give a bunch of grown men kitchen knives? That's the weirdest thing in the world,'" Ruhlin recalls. "Paul saw the look on my face. He said, 'If you do something for the inner circle, everything else in business seems to take care of itself.' At that moment, I realized that Paul understood relationship building at a depth I did not."

So Ruhlin began doing that, too, spending two hundred dollars on a Cutco carving set and engraving the names of the executives he wanted to meet—and their wives—and sending the knives to them. Which then got him the meetings with the CEOs.

He was, mind you, twenty-two years old. The CEOs he met with who were worth a hundred million dollars were expecting a gray-haired executive; instead, they got a spry young buck. But he would land the deal, becoming the largest seller in the country. Ruhlin realized that he had such a gift for gifting that he decided to quit med school and open a gift-giving company. He soon became a sought-after speaker on marketing and relationship building.

Knowing *how* and *when* to give gifts is just as important as *what* to give.

Most people give gifts around a holiday—say, Thanksgiving or Christmas. Usually it's a bottle of wine or fruit basket. That does not fly with Ruhlin. "I don't spend one dime on gifting between Thanksgiving and Christmas, because that's the obligatory time. If you want to connect with people, you want do it just as a surprise. We call it 'Planned Randomness.'"

He takes his Planned Randomness very seriously. In fact, he reinvests 5 to 10 percent of his company's profits back into his relationships. By standing out from the crowd and being remarkable, you'll get noticed. It's not that the gift is so much better than anything anyone else sends during the "normal" time period, but because you are doing the opposite of what is expected.

And that is precisely why he stood out. Rather than send a generic bottle of wine—or knife set—Ruhlin engraved his client's name on it, *along with the client's wife's name*. Not his company name—theirs. "There's never our company name or logo or brand," he says. "Otherwise, it's a promotional product—it's swag—and most people confuse what a gift is and what a marketing tool. As a gift, it's about the recipient, not about you."

He won't send anything consumable unless it's paired with something that's not. The rationale? "If they're thinking about me fifteen years later, then I win," he says. "Top of mind matters. Most people try to remain top of mind with things that are fleeting, but we want people to have something they can use thirty years from now. And the practicality of it is important. Every time they use it, the psychology of reciprocity is really powerful. Most people have in their DNA the pressure to reciprocate. People will take my call ten years later. It plants a seed that doesn't go away."

Not only does he send personalized gifts, but he also sends gifts to people who wouldn't expect to get one—like, say, the CEO's assistant. "If someone sends something I can give to my wife, they get me in the process," he says. "If they make me look cool to my wife and assistant, that's a done deal. People don't realize that it's the people around them or decision makers two executives down who are the most important." These are the people at the top of our Pyramid of Influence.

The Snowblower Effect

We are fans of "surprising and delighting" people whenever possible. (We like to think of it as the kinder, gentler version of "shock and awe.") Every so often, totally at random, we will surprise (and delight!) one of our community members with something completely unexpected. We might send a book that could help them with a project we know they're working on. Or we'll leave an encouraging message for someone we haven't talked to in a while, just to check in.

This serves three purposes: It makes people feel really good to know that there are people out there thinking about them! And it makes us feel good to make them feel good. But also, by offering unexpected value to the people who matter most to us, we are remaining relevant. Every time you "surprise and delight" someone (we are using these words as verbs), it enables you to remain top of mind.

Steve Sims is 100 percent in agreement. Sims recalls the client who was interested in exclusive access to Disney. Sims vaguely knew someone who could help him with this request. As it happens, Sims's contact—the one who might have been able to help him—also desperately craved a Porsche.

Unfortunately, the contact's wife put the kibosh on this idea. In her opinion, the last thing her husband needed was a new Porsche. So Sims, who was born in East London and has the street smarts of a kid born in East London, decided to take matters into his own hands: he sent both this guy and his wife to an exclusive Porsche driving experience to test out cars. As Sims suspected, the wife fell madly in love with the car and relented: her husband was more than welcome to buy his Porsche.

"It cost me $950 for the Porsche driving experience," says Sims. "I can tell you quite openly—the price my client paid for the exclusive access to Disney that this man helped me with was ten times that."

A win-win all around. Not only was his client happy— and Sims got paid handsomely—but Sims also ensured that he would remain in his newfound contact's brain. "I'm embedded in his head," says Sims. "Every time they drive the Porsche, they're thinking of this guy from London." Exactly.

Scott calls this the Snowblower Effect, which came about as the result of an experience he had not long after moving to the New Jersey suburbs in 2015. As we know, Scott is a friendly sort, the kinda guy whom everyone usually knows. But after moving to New Jersey, he realized he knew no one in his neighborhood.

Then winter came, and snow blanketed the town on a repeated basis. Scott dutifully plowed his own driveway. Then he did the neighbors' driveways on each side of him. But why stop there? By the end of the day, Scott had eradicated snow from neighbors on streets in multiple directions. He became the hero of his town, but he also snagged a place in the hearts of all residents. They were ecstatic—and surprised—that someone would be so thoughtful. Not only did he get to know his entire block, but anytime he and his family needed anything, his neighbors were the first to lend a hand.

Teach Someone to Fish . . .

You have probably heard a lot of talk on the value of having a mentor, but you may not have thought about it the way a Superconnector would. By asking for help and guidance—and then living up to and exceeding your mentors' expectations—you can grow your social capital exponentially. Your mentors will take you under their wings and bring you into their various circles (like an anchor, in a sense). Just ask Jared Kleinert.

Jared became an entrepreneur at the ripe old age of fifteen. He admits that when he was trying to build his first company, he made "every single business mistake you can think of." (Imagine!) "But the biggest cardinal sin that I made was having the wrong people around me and having a poor mentor," he says.

Indeed: his mentor at the time was a man he discovered had served time in prison for securities fraud on Wall Street. No fool, Kleinert quickly realized that it would behoove him to surround himself with better people than former white-collar con men. "If you're going to have a mentor, don't make it a bad one," he says wryly.

Not long after, Jared, now sixteen, happened upon an article in *Forbes* called "The Most Connected Man You Don't Know in Silicon Valley." It was about David Hassell, founder and CEO of 15Five, an enterprise software startup based in San Francisco. Kleinert was intrigued. "What struck me about David and how he connected others was not only that all these people went out of their way to hang out with him and to join him at events he put on, but that they also had real change that came into their lives as a result of David," he says.

It was obvious to Jared that David was the type of person he aspired to be like, and so he wrote him a thoughtful cold email, just like that. Boom! After a few back-and-forths, Kleinert offered to work unpaid in exchange for his mentorship. "At sixteen, the only value I could provide really was my time and my energy," he says. "I made it easy for David to say yes."

Kleinert then shaped that role into the "dream internship" he imagined for himself and went from unpaid intern to one of the company's first ten team members. He ultimately helped develop their outbound sales system after some two years of trying almost every other role in the company that didn't involve punching code or executive functions.

But the story doesn't end there. While working for 15Five, Jared met *other* connectors and learned how to become one himself. For example, "I grew up in South Florida," he says. "There's this guy, Eben Pagan, who's one of the top Internet marketers of all time. He's sold more than $100 million worth of information products online and has helped many others to do the same or similar."

Eben was hosting a high-ticket, high-impact conference in Miami that was an hour from where Kleinert grew up.

> David was attending. I went to meet David at the cocktail reception. I wasn't yet able to go to the event, but I joined this cocktail reception. I ended up meeting Eben and a couple of other people in the room whom I still know today. A

few months later, Eben was hosting the same event in Sedona, Arizona. He graciously invited me to join that event. I said yes.

When I went to Eben's event in Sedona, I met another fifty or a hundred other Superconnectors because Eben understands this principle. He was not only surrounding himself with Superconnectors, but also charging them six thousand dollars to get into his event. And everyone was very happy to pay him that. I went. At that event, among other individuals I met was Neil Strauss, who is a *New York Times* best-selling author.

You can imagine what transpired: Kleinert became pals with Strauss. Through a dinner party Strauss threw in Malibu, Jared met Craig Clemens, cofounder of Golden Hippo; adman with more than $1 billion in sales; angel investor to companies like Andela, Snapchat, and Hyperloop One; and "one of the top three copywriters in the world."

From there, Kleinert's gone on to build a network of celebrities, *New York Times* best-selling authors, Fortune 500 executives, professional athletes, international recording artists, Hollywood producers, and many others, just like that.

Incidentally, Kleinert does not think this requires any special talent. "Building meaningful and authentic relationships with high-impact individuals is more approachable than people think," he says. "It doesn't take any sort of special skills or crazy feats of the imagination. I think a few early connections that you treat respectfully and provide value to can really snowball into a very meaningful network for yourself."

Kleinert's story was so amazing that we decided it was worth hearing the other side of it—that would be from David Hassell's perspective. Why did he decide to take a chance on a kid like Kleinert?

Easy. "I was so impressed with this fifteen-year-old kid who was bold enough to reach out in the way that he did," says Hassell. "He was very clear about his desire to learn. He'd done his homework. He was very clear about wanting to learn how to create relationships and what he wanted to do with his career."

What's more, Kleinert worked hard, did what he said he would do, and—most important—built trust. Everyone Hassell introduced him to gave him the thumbs-up.

If you surround yourself with the right mentors and work hard to learn, exceed expectations, and prove yourself reliable and trustworthy, the right mentors often want to take you under their wings and help you succeed. Your success becomes their success.

CHAPTER 6

HABITUAL GENEROSITY

Superconnectors know that their greatest returns come when they least expect them, and by putting others' needs first the good karma seems to flow back to them tenfold. With that insight in mind, Superconnectors are generous with their time and spirit. They derive pleasure from giving. They truly enjoy doing favors for others. Doing something good for other people can only work in their favor.

Superconnectors focus on deep, quality relationships and not those based on "immediate ROI." They look at connections not in terms of "What can I get out of you?" but in terms of "What can I do for you?"

"Most people approach relationships asking what they can get. Instead, they should focus on what they can give," says Adam Rifkin, the cofounder of 106 Miles, a meet-up group that helps technically minded startup entrepreneurs learn from each other. The most successful connectors are givers. According to Rifkin,

They go out of their way to do things for people without asking for anything in return. This builds up a lot of goodwill over time. I built my network one person at a time. Every day I try to do something for someone in my network. Every week I try to meet one new person and understand their needs well enough that I would know whom I should introduce her or him to in the future, if the opportunity arises. Maybe it's offering knowledge; maybe it's offering feedback; maybe it's offering a connection. But it starts with what I have to give.

The most selfish thing you can do is give unselfishly because it always comes back around. I believe that.

The biggest mistake people make about connections, says Keith Ferrazzi, is that they think they have to be reciprocal immediately. "Relationships ebb and flow. When you're at a high point, someone close to you may not be," he says. "How do you help that person get back on track and do it solely to benefit the other person? Don't tally it on an imaginary scoreboard that says, 'I helped Steve fifteen times, but he helped me only eight times. I won't help him again until he catches up.'"

"You can't just measure everything in terms of financial equity," says Linda Rottenberg, the cofounder and CEO of Endeavor, an organization that mentors and accelerates high-impact entrepreneurs in growth markets around the world. "The whole concept of ROI is flawed. You never know what's going to lead to something. Maybe it will in five years. People tend to measure it too soon. People who go in with the attitude of 'I'm doing this to learn, and it might yield nothing!'—those people who are not looking at ROI—tend to gain more. People who look at transactional value only end up earning less."

Most of us are familiar with the concept of paying it forward. It's karmic, really: do good things, and good things will come to you. In Superconnector circles, it's known as the Law of Reciprocity.

In social psychology, reciprocity is a rule that says if someone does something nice for you, you'll feel compelled to do something nice for them. Whatever you call it, the idea is that people will happily repay favors, gifts, or invitations at a later date.

Rifkin swears by something he calls the "Five-Minute Favor," which adds value to someone's life with a favor that takes five minutes or less. "Giving to others when I can, in business and in life, has given my life meaning, and as a result it has brought me happiness, and many great givers I have met in this world share that belief," he says.

What are some of his favorite Five-Minute Favors? Serving as a reference for a person, product, or service. Or sharing or retweeting something on Facebook, Twitter, or LinkedIn. Or sending a real *handwritten* thank-you note for something you are truly grateful for. In fact, when he meets someone new, that's the first thing he thinks about: what he can do for that person. "Maybe it's offering knowledge, maybe it's offering feedback, maybe it's offering a connection, but it starts with what I have to give," he says.

Storytelling

Michael Ellsberg didn't know all the people he wanted to interview for his second book, *The Education of Millionaires*, which included five self-made billionaires and about fifty self-made millionaires who did not go to or finish college, like Sean Parker or Matt Mullenweg. He barely knew any of the people he wanted to interview at the start. He didn't have a big name in the publishing world or author circles yet. He would need to find a way to get connected to these folks.

So how did he meet them? By talking to people. "I had an original topic, a clear point of view on it, and a good platform to be sharing my ideas," he says. "And I just started going to people and doing these interviews. And I would then ask them, 'Do you know anyone else I should interview?'" The more interviews he got, the more people he would meet.

Why did they talk to him? In part, because he presented himself as a storyteller who would help them share their interesting tale with the world. "So these people felt really safe to open up with me and tell me their stories, and they wanted their story told," he says. He was also giving them a forum to share their experiences. "You know society typically judges people who don't go to college, who don't have a college degree. And a lot of these people actually still, despite all their success, have that little check mark in their minds that hasn't been checked off and are feeling a bit of perhaps shame around it. I was offering them a chance to reframe that whole narrative to be a source of value rather than a source of shame, and I think people are really excited by that opportunity."

But there also was a power of association at play. Initially, he could only pitch people on the concept. He had a book deal with a reputable publisher (Penguin), but he didn't have any other names. But once he had five or six interviews done, he could name names: "Yes, I'd like to feature your story alongside the story of Matt Mullenweg, the cofounder of WordPress. I'd like to feature your story next to that of David Gilmour, the lead guitarist of Pink Floyd. I'd like to feature your story next to, you know, Sean Parker's, the cofounding president of Facebook."

Ellsberg was offering a win-win situation: people could share their stories alongside some of the most powerful people in the world. Hard to turn that down.

When you help to share the stories of others—on blogs, books, or other media—the right questions and quality platforms stand out to those individuals you may wish to meet. Building or creating a platform that resonates with a tribe can create a lot of value when you're looking to connect with other people.

The last thing you want to be is the Forrest Gump of the Internet. Which is to say, you don't want your name popping up in every digital nook and cranny. You need to pick and choose the areas in which you want to be known. Be strategic.

Four years ago, Lewis Howes began hosting a podcast called *The School of Greatness*, based on his best-selling book, which became hugely popular. So reputation is something he often thinks about. He freely admits that he originally put it out there for "selfish reasons"—to "get information from the things that I wanted to learn from these brilliant people that I wanted to interview, and then also to be able to share that information with the world because I felt like most people don't have the information that I was learning from these individuals," he says.

Over time, he realized that he had interviewed hundreds of people whom he had promoted online, talking to them about the things they cared most about. He has also benefited: those same people have promoted his business and books.

Howes puts a lot of thought and energy into his podcast. He researches the hell out of each guest, so he understands what makes them tick and what excites them most. "I'm very particular about the guests I have on and the information that we share," he says. "And I say no to a lot of people because I want it to be the highest-quality content that I can put out there because that's a reflection of me, whatever I put out there. And also, if it's average content, people aren't going to listen to it or watch it or read it, so I'm always looking to produce the best content and the best quality, and that means I need to develop myself with better skills and tools to tap into someone's information even better so that the content is the best it can be."

Howes conducts each interview in person, not by phone or Skype. And he asks the subject a number of questions before they begin.

A mainstay: Is anything off-limits? They usually say no. Then he asks, is it okay to take the conversation anywhere it naturally goes? "By doing that, the energy shifts, their attitude shifts, and they're like, 'Oh, okay, this is for real,'" he says. "This is not just some, like, canned PR-response type of interview that I'm going to do; this is for me. I'm really going to go somewhere."

He gets consistent credibility through association, a way to meet new and amazing people, and reliable high-quality content that he can share, all of which plays on a number of levels. His digital footprint is solid and attracts the right kinds of people for his professional goals.

Incidentally, we have spoken with many people for this book, many of whom we did not know at all when we started.

After each interview, we asked the person we were talking to if he or she could recommend someone else they thought should be in here and then introduce us. You are holding the result of those introductions in your hands.

The Human Tollbooth

Every good connector needs to be smack in the center of his or her universe. Being at the center allows you to see and hear things from different perspectives, to become more worldly (in a professional sense), and, as a result, to become exponentially more valuable since you are, in effect, a human tollbooth. If anyone wants to cross to the other side, they have to go through you. This is a good place to be.

Jeremy Fiance is the founder and managing partner of The House Fund, the first venture capital (VC) fund focused on Berkeley. (Not to make you feel bad, but he cofounded five startup organizations with friends while a student there.)

Fiance graduated from UC Berkeley at the end of 2014. As a freshman, he set out to find resources for a venture he wanted to start. But he couldn't find anything. This surprised him—Berkeley is close to Silicon Valley, after all. But nope, nothing existed.

So he decided to create the world he wished already existed. He ended up starting the Berkeley chapter of the Kairos Society, a collegiate entrepreneurship organization, with the aim of building a community that others were looking for. "I was very passionate about bringing people together," he says. By the time he graduated, the organizations he started sparked fifty startups that had raised more than $50 million in funding. Fiance is a human tollbooth because everyone has to go through him. He has successfully bridged the gap between the university world and the venture capital world.

"I have a genuine interest in learning about other humans and a genuine curiosity in learning about many different areas," he says.

> Just being willing to listen and willing to help other folks is surprisingly something many people aren't used to. I took an active approach in getting to know people in the startup world or had interest in it, and that's something many folks just don't do.
>
> Most people think about the goal that's right in front of them. But I try to look at relationships from a long-term perspective. That aligns well with venture capital, since it takes a while to see a company be successful. Certain people may be helpful over the course of many years. I think of it as unlocking the right connections at the right time.

Becoming a more generous person, and, eventually, a habitually generous person, can be achieved only with practice. Set daily affirmations for yourself to go an inch further than most people would. For example, if someone meets you for coffee at your behest, send them a handwritten thank-you note or a five-dollar gift card to pay for their next cup of coffee rather than a simple email.

Small gestures like this go a long way and can help you work yourself up to bigger, more inspirational moments the likes of Ruhlin and others. But for today, keep it simple. You can't run until you learn how to walk.

CHAPTER 7

HOW TO COMMUNICATE WITH ANYONE, ANYTIME, ANYWHERE, ABOUT ANYTHING

Connectors communicate in very specific ways. Rather than just breaking into conversation, they combine critical thinking and pointed ways of speaking and listening in order to quickly learn about people. The goal is to build deeper relationships with real context, beyond surface level, while also assessing how they can add value. This means they must listen. And ask the right questions. And analyze and plan ahead. And ask more questions.

A connector's goal is to get as much context on the other person through conversation, research, surroundings, and third parties. Context is important, because it helps you create a profile of an individual and also helps you determine your next steps, so you're not operating blindly.

The best Superconnectors uncover context, data, and specificity through conversation. They're like the Sherlock Holmes of Discourse, peeling back layers of jargon, uncertainty, or inconsistencies to determine the true value that can be unleashed with the right connection or resource. Take the example of Jon Levy, who wanted to lead an exceptional life. He didn't know how he was going to achieve this goal; he just knew that somehow, in some way, he was going to.

At the time of this realization, he was twenty-eight years old, working in middle management, making a decent living but not feeling like he was doing anything remarkable. Then he went to a personal success seminar called "Wisdom Unlimited," conducted by Landmark Education, and that is where he had his epiphany. "I was sitting there, and the leader said, 'The fundamental element that defines the quality of your life is the people you surround yourself with and the conversations you have with them,'" Levy, now thirty-six, recalls. "I really took that to heart. All of us know this is true, but very few of us live our lives that way. We don't curate the people around us. I said to myself, 'What would it take to curate the people around me?'"

He started looking at the behavior of influential people and tried to understand what would have them engage with a stranger. He decided he needed to do something novel. "I'm a strong believer that if you want to connect to people, one of the most effective ways is to work on a task with them so you have a common goal," he says. "I could get them to bond by creating something that nourished them, that stood outside the normal range."

And in New York City, where he lived, that meant . . . cooking. Yes, he would invite a group of strangers over to his house and have them whip up a meal together. He would buy the ingredients; they would each be paired on a cooking task with someone they never met before. They would then eat together, and the conversation would flow.

No one knows what anyone else does for a living, and they are not allowed to discuss their work until the very end of the evening. This way they actually have to get to know each other, and no one is thinking about "who they should know in the room" or "titles." Or that it's the same simple meal each time. Or that he keeps pairing different people together to share remedial tasks so they end up concentrating on conversation. (He was smart enough to get them to clean up for him, too.)

It was a genius idea, but there was one thing standing between him and a place mat: he didn't actually know the people he wanted to invite. He wanted to hobnob with Nobel laureates, Olympic athletes, business executives. They were not (not at the time, anyway) part of his inner circle.

But why let a mere technicality stand in his way? He devoted about thirty hours a week to his project, planning, organizing, and researching possible guests. Then he had to go about actually communicating with them.

He compiled a list of hundreds of names and confirmed twelve—thinkers, artists, media moguls—and then invited them over. Most of them were his core circle. His first dinner was in 2009. Seven years and more than a hundred meals later, Levy, who calls himself a "human behavioral scientist" and is the author of *The 2 AM Principle*, now holds twice-monthly meals in New York, San Francisco, and LA. To replenish the guest list, "I asked for recommendations, and I kept collecting names and contact information from people I met," he says.

Since his guests were bonding over a shared activity—cooking—they built more than business relationships: they became friends. And better than that: they became *his* friends.

Forbes heard about it and approached him for an article. The *New York Times* followed suit, and other media came calling. This gave him the freedom to cold-email people he wanted to meet in the future. When he wanted to sell his book, one of his influencers introduced him to a hotshot agent, who quickly sold the book. He's now in talks with a production company that wants to acquire the rights and also make TV shows about his community members. And it all arose from the relationships he had.

Clearly, nothing happened by chance; he created his network, and he's still creating it. He passes their names to industry experts, who give them either the thumbs-up or the thumbs-down.

Meeting While Introverted (MWI)

You might think that most great connectors are inherently extroverted people: gregarious, life-of-the-party sorts of people. In fact, there's a lot of evidence to suggest the opposite.

Don't be afraid if you aren't a laugh a minute. Some people estimate that introverts constitute one-third to half of the US population. Many are terrific Superconnectors. Everyone needs to learn how to have a conversation, whether they are introverted or extroverted. The content doesn't change; the strategies to get there do. Introverted Superconnectors don't hide;

they simply play to their personality type. They figure out what works best for them and then use it to the maximum effect. Play to your strengths.

A Type A personality—that is, someone like Scott, who isn't shy, who feeds off other people, who loves meeting new folks—can just walk up to someone and start a conversation. Ryan finds this somewhat challenging.

So Ryan gathers smaller groups of people together. At our annual entrepreneurial ski retreat for YEC, he makes it a point to try to take a lift up the mountain with every single member who attends. "It's my chance at one-on-one time, away from the herd," he says. "I learn more about that person during that short ride back to the top of the mountain than I will for the rest of the weekend."

Or else he meets people online before taking the relationships offline, much like Dan Schawbel does. Some of Ryan's closest colleagues were people he met in his early twenties blogging on Employee Evolution. Many of them were introverts, and the blogosphere gave them a place to share their ideas—however brazen they might be—without all of the anxiety that might come from communicating the same wild ideas to people in real life. "Those connections became some of my closest professional colleagues and lifelong friends, many of whom I turn back to for help every time we launch a new community at The Community Company," says Ryan.

According to Susan Cain, the lawyer turned revolutionary author of the book *Quiet*, about the power of introverts, Ryan is behaving exactly as he should. Cain came to her subject from personal experience—she is a self-described introvert and knows that she is different from the cultural ideal. "I was always very aware that our social structures were set up for people who were quite extroverted and that introverts were asked to put on an extroverted mask when they went out in public," she says. "And then it would be like, 'Oh, okay, come home and be your true self.'"

Cain has forgotten the whole concept of "networking" and instead walks through the world in search of kindred spirits. "You know when you've found those people. You know when you've met somebody who you feel like 'Oh, yeah, I get her. She gets me. I really want to be helpful' or 'We're on the same wavelength over here.'"

Cain suggests people give themselves an informal quota. Once you've met one or two kindred spirits, you are allowed to leave the event and hole up in your hotel room. But remember to "cultivate those people and really stay in touch with them," she says. "That's so much more valuable than a series of awkward conversations."

Cain's father was a doctor and medical school professor, and her grandfather was a rabbi. They gave great credence to those who don't have big, boisterous personalities. Because of her family, she believes that introverts "have a lot of power and a lot to contribute to the world."

> Introverts tend to be deep and reflective thinkers. They tend to be really good at creative stuff. I don't think it's because they necessarily have some mysterious gene for creativity, but rather that creativity actually requires time spent alone, and introverts are good at that.

My philosophy of life is that, regardless of what you say, people can feel what you feel about them. It comes through in a million different ways that I think we're mostly not even aware of. So if you're operating sincerely with people and you do care about them, whether you're in touch at that moment or not, they know that.

Some people aren't sure if they are an introvert or extrovert. Cain has a test you can take on her website, quietrev.com, and it's really valuable. Because (once again) self-knowledge is key. It's important to know who you really are. She asks,

Is your idea of a great day sitting at a café or taking a long walk? Is it going out with one close friend, which is probably more of an introverted tendency? Is it hey, let me get together with my best friends from college whom I haven't seen in a while? You know, let's go out, all eight of us? You can see pretty quickly. And then ask yourself, okay, what if I had a week of Saturdays, with absolutely no obligations, how would I spend my time over the course of that week? You start figuring out who you are. The point of this exercise is to become conscious of how many of your actions are dictated by social obligation and not by your true preferences. You get to know yourself better.

There are a number of other online quizzes to help with the process. One of our favorites is from the *Harvard Business Review* (https://hbr.org/2015/06/quiz-yourself-do-you-lead-with -emotional-intelligence).

The Value of Weak Ties

Adam Rifkin, the CEO and cofounder of PandaWhale, an Internet service for consuming, saving, and organizing content found on the Web and social networks, is also an introvert. Wharton professor and best-selling author Adam Grant dubbed him the "Kevin Bacon of Silicon Valley."

One of the ways Rifkin has built successful relationships is by reestablishing contact with people he once knew rather than jumping right in to build new relationships. Invariably, they'll be more receptive than those you have to meet fresh and new. "I build relationships a little bit at a time," says Rifkin, who is also the cofounder of 106 Miles, a meet-up group whose purpose is to help technically minded startup entrepreneurs learn from each other. "By reconnecting with someone, you can catch up on what they've been working on and what they're looking forward to, and this allows you to build deeper relationships by looking for opportunities to help them."

Say you were in a fraternity in college or worked at a company with them fifteen years ago. No one—especially not in today's connect-with-everybody climate—is going to think it odd if you reach out with a friendly "What have you been up to?" or "How are things?" Chances are, they'll be just as interested in hearing what you've been doing. More important: you never know where rekindling these relationships may lead.

Grant refers to them as "dormant ties." Most people are more comfortable reaching out to people they already know than sidling up to a stranger. It's a natural jumping-off point and will lead to the same end results over time: new people.

You build associations and affiliation with your preestablished network who then push you forward as a result.

Stanford professor and sociologist Mark Granovetter noted in a 1973 study that people are 58 percent more likely to get a new job through a "weak" tie. Nineteen percent went the more traditional route, through a job listing or executive recruiter.

Adam Grant wondered how this was possible in a June 2013 LinkedIn post, "Finding the Hidden Value in Your Network." The logical answer, he noted, is that we have more weak than strong ties, so the odds are greater that a weak tie would provide assistance. But there was another explanation, too: "Strong ties tend to give us redundant knowledge," he wrote. "Our closest contacts tend to know the same people and information as we do. Weak ties travel in different circles and learn different things, so they can offer us more efficient access to novel information." Most of us associate with people with similar outlooks and perspectives, so we aren't learning anything new.

The problem is that most people aren't comfortable reaching out to strangers to ask for help. But Grant realized that there was a third type of tie: a "dormant tie," the people you *used* to know, whom you may not have spoken to in years. It could be "a childhood neighbor, a college roommate, or a colleague from your first job," says Grant. These people have invariably become friendly with other people they can introduce you to. But since you have a shared history, they're a step (or three) up from a mere acquaintance.

Of course, not every person you've ever crossed paths with is worth revisiting. But many are. And these people will probably be eager to engage in conversation with you, because there is already an in there. There is history. Context.

Rifkin is a staunch believer in what he calls the "Five Email" rule. "If you lost your job tomorrow, besides your parents, who would you send your first five emails to?" he asks. "Who are the people from your past you need to invest the most time in to bring them into your present?"

That was the premise behind 106 Miles, which has thousands of members. People meet once or twice a month in a social setting, and there are no speakers. "Instead, members just talk with each other about what they're working on and ask each other questions to learn from each other," he says.

Reconnecting can be done online via email or social media, but Rifkin believes it's more effective if you meet offline. (We agree, although we have plenty of people in our network whom we have never met in person. They are very valuable and important assets.)

Grant ultimately added a reminder to his calendar, telling him to reconnect with at least one dormant tie each month. (Most people can be easily found on LinkedIn.) Any excuse is valid, he says: calling to wish someone a happy birthday or reaching out when visiting an old friend's city. "Let people know that they really mattered in your life, you miss interacting, and you'd love to reconnect," he says.

But instead of asking them for help, "I've been searching for ways to help them—sometimes by sharing knowledge, in other cases by making introductions," he says. "In my experience, rekindling old connections has become a source of meaning and happiness. Like renovating an old house, it brings us the best of the old and the new. Our dormant ties can help us revitalize our favorite features of our past selves, while opening doors to new future selves."

Context, Context, Context

To be successful at connecting, you must create a full profile of the person you are talking to. You want to determine who this person really is. You're also determining if they're an okay person or an "amazing" person whom you would want to invest considerable time and energy in over the years.

Most people think of life in black and white terms. Connectors are more interested in the gray zones, in the subtle nuances that make us all unique. What are the other person's likes and dislikes, the things you don't find on their Facebook or LinkedIn profiles? If someone says to you, "I like asparagus," the proper response is not "Great!" but "Why? What is it about those skinny green stalks that speaks to you?"

Your goal in any conversation is to go beyond surface level, to get context and find out something remarkable about the person that will help you remember them later on. *You hold the world record for underwater breathing? Amazing! How'd you get into that?*

Superconnectors size people up, not to feel morally superior or because they might not make introductions above their "financial" or executive status (e.g., introducing a newbie to a titan of industry), but because *they* need to know. You need to keep all of these things in the back of your head, to figure out who the person is and what they are looking for. You need all the information in your quiver, so you can act accordingly.

Take Steve Sims, whom we met earlier. Sims, if you recall, is a Superconcierge. He's the dude who Makes Things Happen. If you want to meet the pope, or go to the Oscars, or take a private sub around the *Titanic*, he's your guy. Not surprisingly, his job is all about leveraging relationships: knowing, and remembering, people. This also includes knowing what they are all about and caring about them. It means not just asking them what they do but also wondering: *What are you about? What are your hobbies? What interests you? What's your thesis?* "My entire business is about how to get the most out of a situation, how to get people to buy into what I want to and have it be a win for them," says Sims. "I'm a great believer in relationship over network."

To Sims, building relationships is like growing vegetables. "You need to nourish everything," he says. "Nurture it. You need to put the effort in. If I'm going to connect with you, the only way I'm going to do that is by learning your likes and dislikes. What propels you? So I build up a profile of what makes you beat. 'What do you do in your free time? Where would you go? Oh, you like racing cars? What kind?' When you can get into that, it's no longer forced."

Not every conversation will be life changing. Nor do you have to agree with everyone you meet on every subject. Some of Scott's closest friends have radically different political views than he does. But so what? You don't have to be aligned on every point. It doesn't matter that you're a Republican and the person you are talking to is a die-hard Democrat. More important is why you each feel the way you do. The context.

Imagine you're at a party and you meet someone for the first time. You notice them drinking WhistlePig 15 Year. You discover that, in fact, bourbon is their all-time favorite drink. That's a great detail and one that might very well come in handy at a later date. Now you know something about this person that's not on their LinkedIn profile. It's *specific* information. "You are learning something about the *person*," says Sims. "You are building context and your own profile that's your own private war chest of information."

To pad his war chest, right after he meets someone new, Sims writes down bullet points of interesting factoids he learned. He doesn't do this in some highly complex customer relationship management (CRM) software, by the way, but in the notes section of his address book! An example:

Joseph Blowseph:

- Met at Mashable rooftop bar event at SXSW
- Likes WhistlePig, Bob Dylan, Formula One
- Has twin sons
- Does capoeira
- Grew up in Chicago
- Currently reading García Márquez

"People can talk about their lusts and loves and hobbies all day long," says Sims.

Invariably, Sims walks away with a trove of information. But there have been moments when he has struck out, when he has encountered people he just can't crack. And you know what he does when that happens? He cuts the conversation off after forty-five seconds. That's right: he shakes their hand and moves on. "You don't need long to get bored senseless," he says. (Forty-five seconds, incidentally, is longer than you might think. Sims likens it to a minute-and-a-half round of kickboxing. "Come in the ring with me, and you tell me that's not a bloody long time," he says.)

At our company, The Community Company, we get similar intel on all of our prospective hires. Ryan conducts the final interview, but it's not the typical Q&A most HR managers do. Ryan's not interested in skill set—that's the easy part. Our team has meticulous ways of gauging an applicant's skills. By the time Ryan meets up with them, they've already been vetted. Ryan is there to suss out the other information, the things most HR managers don't ask.

"I request a 'freestyle' about who they are as a person," he says. "'What do you like? More important, what do you *not* like? What do you do outside of work that defines you? How do you think working for our company is going to enhance that identity? What kind of relationships do you keep close to you?' I ask these things because it helps me understand how well they will fit in our company culture, if they fit at all; how our managers should support their growth; and what their best motivators are going to be."

One of our managers once said that it was "the coolest and weirdest interview" she'd ever been on. But she left feeling like "This is where I'm meant to be." (We hired her.)

When we talk about context, we are looking for not just context *about* the person but also context *around* them—the visual and environmental cues that go beyond the words they say. Say you are meeting someone at a fancy cocktail party. Well, who brought them there, and what's their relationship to one another? What are they drinking? How are they dressed? Some cues will be very useful, others less so. But these types of things help you build a profile on this person or help you restart conversations with people you've met before.

And in an era where most of us never leave home without some kind of mobile device, it's simple to jot down a few notes after a conversation, just like Steve Sims does.

Redefining Small Talk

Now that you have a little bit of background on this person, you're faced with Challenge Number 2: *How the hell do you talk to them in a meaningful way?* How do you know which questions to ask or the best follow-up questions? How do you hone your listening skills to ensure your understanding of the subject matter and the applicable context? And finally, how do you do all this while thinking about what or who you might know who may be able to provide assistance or answers? By turning everyday "small talk" into "context conversation."

Small talk makes the world go 'round. Without it, how would you know if the person you're talking to likes hot or cold weather or if they prefer *Ghostbusters* to *Caddyshack?* The main reason small talk even exists is to catch up, break the ice, and have a benign, pleasant conversation. When you have nothing else to talk about, you pull a few gems out of your hat that anyone can answer. (See *Ghostbusters*, above.) Above all else, small talk is pleasant.

So it's no wonder that most people go with what's safe and easy. They don't know the right questions to ask or how to probe in a respectful manner to uncover the real need.

But not connectors! Connectors never make meaningless small talk. Connectors have small talk with a *purpose*. They are never just engaging in conversation for the sake of conversation. They always have a clear goal in mind: to extract the most pointed and relevant information about the other person. Connectors don't have casual conversations just to kill time. They are probing for a reason—to see what this person is all about, to create context for a profile that they can use later.

Whenever we talk with someone new, we never walk away thinking, "What a great chat." Rather, what's coursing through our minds is "How can I provide strategic value for you, even if you're not asking me to right now?"

This latter point is significant, because you never know when someone might come back to you with a request and how you will be able to help them out. Okay, fine, you say. It's one thing to talk to someone in a similar place in life as you are. But what happens if you're meeting a high-ranking official? How do you talk to them without feeling overwhelmed and intimidated?

An excellent question, one we've wrestled with ourselves when we were first starting out. We've met everyone from CEOs of Fortune 500 companies to the president of the United States, and it can be daunting. And terrifying.

But at the end of the day, they're just people. Sure, they might have more money or power than you, but they all started out as babies, learned to walk, went to fifth grade, graduated high school, and made mistakes. You need to undress the executive titles, the social media–follower counts, and all of the other decor, even if you're talking to the president. Get to the core of who they are. Pretend they're just like your mother or father. Because they are.

Remember the old trope that if you have a fear of public speaking, you should imagine the members of the audience naked? (It was highlighted in a *Brady Bunch* episode.) This is a similar idea. If you believe that we are all the same—that no one is any better or worse than anyone else—then everyone is fair game. With a few exceptions—say, children of billionaires or royal families, who grew up with silver spoons firmly planted in their mouths—most of us started off similarly.

Scott's wife, Tana, is an incredibly talented paper artist and founder of Bohemian Bloom. She has designed paper flora for Harry Winston and the White House and has also done invitations for celebrities. One of her heroes is Martha Stewart. Not long ago, Tana was given the opportunity to meet her. She leaped at the chance, of course: this was her idol, Martha Freaking Stewart! But she was also terrified. What would they talk about? What if she said something stupid or clammed up?

She needn't have worried. Martha Stewart is a genuine person who cares about artists. She asked Tana specific questions about her work; the conversation was organic and familiar, and Tana's angst disappeared. Once it was clear that there was a commonality and they shared like-minded interests, a natural conversation ensued.

If you approach a celebrity or public figure as a fan, you'll be treated like one. Their guard goes up; so many people want something from them. So if you treat a celebrity like a celebrity, you should prepare for a minimal, surface-level exchange that's likely to last a fraction of a moment. But if you treat them

like a person—a real person, who eats and sleeps and poops—
the likelihood of a real, context-rich exchange increases. People want to be treated like regular people, even if they don't
admit it publicly. Most people want to have a conversation, too.
They're often just afraid to.

Had Tana treated Martha as a celebrity mogul rather than a
doyenne of the arts, they would not have had such a meaningful
chat. When she realized that the Empress was just a nice woman
from Nutley, New Jersey, the conversation became fluid and easy.

In the end, Martha kept one of Tana's pieces of art for her
desk. That's real estate that money can't buy.

As an exercise, whether you end up doing so or not later
on, you should always be able to walk away from every conversation and immediately be able to introduce that person to
someone else, citing multiple factoids you have learned. But
you want to do so in a thoughtful manner.

The wrong way: "Hey, Jack, have you met John? He's great."

The right way: "Hey, Jack, have you met John? He's an am-
ateur dancer in his spare time and a very accomplished artist who's having his next show in a few weeks. We were just
talking about the cheese and wine choices. You own a restaurant. What's your suggestion?"

Again, not only is the context you get helpful for your arsenal, but your ability to use it will humanize your introductions,
reaffirm your care and listening skills, and start off the next
"context conversation" between other parties with success.
This accomplishes multiple goals simultaneously. It's a faster,
stronger engagement, and it positions you as the person who is
Always in the Know.

CHAPTER 8

GOOD QUESTIONS, BAD QUESTIONS, AND EVERYTHING IN BETWEEN

Good questions are those that keep people talking and offering up more context. Good questions are open-ended. They do not end with yes or no—this is, after all, an exercise in *conversation*, not a game of True or False. Good questions are natural jumping-off points for future discussions. Superconnectors train themselves to have conversations that fill in ask gaps. In short, good questions keep people talking about what matters to them rather than making traditional, obligatory small talk.

While people are talking about the things they need, we're racking our brains around what or who we know who could provide value in some way. We're trying to find natural fits based on our investigation, so we can solve the puzzle.

Why "How Can I Help You?"
Is the Worst. Question. Ever.

A Superconnector's job is to lead a conversation through questions. But you don't want to barrage people with inquiries or make them feel like they're testifying before the House Un-American Activities Committee. You want to start with little icebreakers, the sorts of queries that encourage natural chatter. You want them to feel comfortable opening up, not about a trauma from their adolescence but about something pertaining to their current situation.

We used to think that "How can I help you?" was the perfect question for this—direct, to the point, and easy to answer, especially since most people don't know how to ask for help. But we were wrong! (Have we mentioned that humility is one of a Superconnector's greatest strengths?)

"How can I help you?" is a really crappy catchphrase that could very well make you lose credibility in the eyes of the person you are talking to, especially if it's early on in your relationship-building process with that individual. In fact, it might just be the worst question you could possibly ask.

Why? Because "How can I help you?" is broad and unclear. It also assumes that the other person is already sold on the fact that you're a helpful person to know. Finally, and perhaps most important, today the phrase has been espoused by so many blogs and gurus, it feels stale and icky and screams "marketing tactic!" It's another one of those concepts that started with great intentions, but like every other platform or tool that worked, people found a way to turn it into sales-speak or a code word for "Let me ask if you need anything, so it won't 'seem' sleazy or off-putting when I immediately ask you for something right afterward" or "when I make you feel awkward if you don't ask me the same question, which is actually my real intent."

Vanessa Van Edwards, the professional people watcher we met earlier, feels similarly about that question, as well as "What do you do?" "It's a social script," she says. "We answer as if it's memorization. If people like what they do, they'll find a way to tell you about it. If they don't, they'll find a way to avoid it, and that's the best thing you can learn about someone."

However, Van Edwards found that asking "What are you working on?" gets amazing responses. People light up like the electric grid when you ask them that. They lean in toward her and visibly animate. Not only does "What are you working on?" sound more like a casual conversation, but it also puts you in the driver's seat to listen and discover opportunities where you can provide value. "The sweet spot is finding conversation starters that are easy to access," she says.

Reminder: You are not there to talk about yourself. You are trying to learn what the other person is about. This doesn't mean you just pepper them with questions, but it means you aren't there to wax poetic about yourself and your many accomplishments. Eventually, you won't even realize you're doing it. It will come naturally to you.

Again, if a question ends with a yes or no statement, then you have not done your job.

Why Good Questions Matter

Most people suck at asking for help, and when they do ask, they are unable to articulate what they need in a clear, concise, and action-oriented way. We can't tell you how often we meet people who have a totally different ask from what they initially say.

At YEC we receive a lot of requests to partner. We regularly receive emails from people who say, "I'd love to partner with YEC. Let's talk about how."

Um, okay. But what exactly does that mean? Do you want us to give you money to sponsor your event? Provide us your service at a discount? What do you want to partner on? Can you give us a clue? Usually, we hit delete faster than you can say . . . Superconnector.

In effect, Superconnectors are trying to solve a series of puzzles or help someone reach the end of a maze. As we have discussed, Superconnectors ask questions and talk with purpose in order to uncover context and value that can help the person they're speaking to—knowing that the person they're speaking to is not necessarily clear about what they need or what would best help them.

A need, by the way, can be in the form of a connection that leads to a business or personal relationship, insights/knowledge/education, or a vendor/tool/resource. It is your job as a Superconnector to figure out whom you know who can fill these various needs.

Questions are audience specific. Are you talking to a young upstart who's counting every penny or a serial entrepreneur worth millions? Are they a CEO or in middle management? Are they clear and concise or unfocused and scattered?

If you *have* met before—say, at a business event six months earlier—then it helps to reference the place. If you can say you've met before and give one quick data point, you're adding an extra layer of trust to the foundation. You can gain instant credibility with this person if you are able to say when you last saw them and the remarkable thing you learned about them. This type of thing stands out, creating and solidifying an impression. (Now, you probably meet many people in your life, and you truly might not remember small details. That's why it's important to build great systems to help you remember key insights about them. It doesn't have to be some complex CRM system—Steve Sims jots down notes in his phone. We will get into this in greater depth later on.)

For example, "When we met at the National Bricklayers Association annual convention, you were talking about the addition to your house. How's that going?" or "Last we spoke you were heading to China. What was your favorite part of the trip?"

We don't see this as Machiavellian, by the way. We're not trying to pull the wool over anyone's eyes; we are genuinely trying to help them. We are translating their words into data and turning that data into an analysis.

Now, what happens if you haven't met the person before? Then you are, in theory, starting fresh. It's all new. Ask away! It's all fair game.

Making Digital Outreach Human

What happens when you, the connector, want to reach out to someone you've never met? Is it kosher to reach out of the blue? Yes. But again, there is protocol. There is very much a right way—and a wrong way—to do this.

The wrong way is what we all have seen and can't stand: promotional, self-serving messaging or messages poorly masked as nonpromotional messaging. Getting involved in existing threads just to make your own points, instead of actually taking in what the original post says and responding more appropriately. Using market- or sales-speak instead of humanspeak to sound "more professional" or smart. Or, as is most common in standard cold outreach, immediately asking to connect offline with them via phone or an in-person meeting without putting in the time in the channel that they care about to show your genuine caring and value before trying to force them to your preferred meeting channel.

Now let's get to the right ways.

Make a Cold Outreach Hot

You're not always going to meet the people who will be meaningful to you in person. Sometimes, you might have to email someone out of the blue. This is not easy; we know. But it can be done!

Here is a step-by-step guide from Jared Kleinert, who is the Master of the Cold Email. Kleinert, if you remember, sent a cold email to David Hassell, who became his mentor. He went from knowing no one to being called the "Most Connected Millennial" by *USA Today* and building an entire consulting practice one relationship at a time. His first client? Keith Ferrazzi, number-one *New York Times* best-selling author of business-book classic *Never Eat Alone* (on professional relationship building—go figure) and former CMO of Deloitte and Starwood Hotels, whom Kleinert also emailed out of the blue.

• **Start with a catchy subject line.** Make it as to the point as possible or make it social proof as much as possible. The subject line of the cold email he sent out to Keith Ferrazzi: "18-year-old, TEDx speaker, author-to-be looking to provide value." It was about what Kleinert could offer Ferrazzi and also showed that he had the street cred of being a TEDx speaker and an author to be (he'd already inked a deal for his first book with St. Martin's Press, which went on to become the "#1 Entrepreneurship Book of 2015," according to Axiom Business Book Awards, when Kleinert was only nineteen years old).

• **Keep the message short.** A quick "Hi so and so" will suffice. In one sentence you can say the specific reason you're reaching out and how you want to help them. Your first line should be something about how you can provide value to them. "You should have done your research ahead of time to know what they have going on that you can be of help with," he says. "The worst thing you could do is ask how I can help because then it forces the other person to think of something that you can help with, and they have no idea who you are. You want to do your research ahead of time and then offer something timely." With Ferrazzi, Kleinert knew exactly what he wanted: *I want to help you with your upcoming book launch* (*Never Eat Alone: Expanded and Updated* was about to be released). *I also want to help you grow your speaking business using the outbound sales methodology of a VC-backed startup in Silicon Valley.*

• **Be transparent with your goals and motives.** If you want to help someone, in part, because it's going to be a great learning experience for a similar situation that you have coming up, then state that in as short a way as possible. Offer that first sentence or two as strictly how you provide value. The rest of that or the middle part of that email should really be about your social proof, meaning, have you been quoted in any media outlets?

• **Give "social proof."** Have you worked with or done this sort of work with similar people in the industry? You want to show that you're not just any random person reaching out to them.

• **Offer a very specific call to action.** Be direct, to the point: "Can we hop on a fifteen-minute phone call on this day at this time?" "I like to give them options as well so that you avoid the back-and-forth of 'I can't do this time, but I can do that time. What about you?'" Kleinert states. "I'll say, 'Can you do this time on this day? If not, how about these other two times?' That's how I'll close my email. If it's not a schedule or meeting request, you want to offer another clear call to action."

• **Have a clear-cut email signature.** You want to make sure to tout any accomplishments in your signature. Kleinert's says "Entrepreneur, award-winning author, TED speaker." "It makes mention of the fact that I was named 'USA *Today*'s Most Connected Millennial' and that I was named a 'Champion for Humanity,' by the United Nations," he points out. "These are things that make you sound like a total asshole if you were stating them aloud at a party. If you put it in your email signature, which is known to be a very important and often overlooked part of someone's email, it's the perfect place where you can put social proof and keep your emails pretty short."

If someone doesn't respond to him in three days, he'll normally send them a follow-up. He will follow up one more time, usually a week after the original point of contact. Maybe four days after that, he'll send a third and final note. "I'll either say something as short as 'Following up' or 'Checking in,'" says Kleinert. "If I'm in a more playful mood, I will find a GIF online. I will copy and paste that into my email. I think that's fun. I don't see any reason to be stuffy and not playful in today's world. Life is short. We are allowed to be as weird and authentic in business as we want, more so than ever before."

Incidentally, he does not use bitmojis. He hates them, "simply because my mom and my grandma use them." Fair enough. This ties nicely into our last point.

• **Connect with people using the language of whatever platform you are on.** We don't market or look to "growth hack" follower counts or overshare what we ate for breakfast. We use these platforms to create collision digitally, build inroads with people we haven't met or can't meet in person, and bring these exchanges into in-person or longer-form private digital conversations that ultimately lead to the same results as emails or in-person meetings would—context conversations that have the opportunity to become deep relationships.

Social Media

Obviously, you can spend hours on Facebook trying to perfect your Words with Friends score. But if you compare the amount of time you might waste at a random "networking event" where you don't know if you'll walk away having met anyone interesting versus spending a few hours on a social networking site where you're researching people in a field you're interested in connecting with and liking their posts and eventually writing them—well, it kinda puts it all in perspective.

"People are still people, so they still respond to the same incentives, and they still want to work with people they know, like, and trust," says Ferrazzi. "What's changed is the technology by which we connect. Social media makes connecting with people all over the world possible, and there are networking apps that help you find people who share your interests. We're not limited to schlepping down to a meeting hall or hotel conference room, hoping to make those connections. Not that there's anything wrong with schlepping down to meet someone face-to-face."

How to Engage in Other People's Threads and Posts

Michael Ellsberg, author of *The Education of Millionaires: It's Not What You Think and It's Not Too Late*, purposefully injects himself into different comment-section conversations on social media. "I love social networking platforms for connecting with people," he says. "If you tweet out an interesting response or share an article or someone asks a question and you have a good response, you can get into a dialogue with people you would never have had access to otherwise."

He also points out that having your own online platform and content effectively does your networking for you. For example, he became friends with Neil Strauss, the best-selling author, who reached out to Ellsberg after reading one of his articles. "He reached out and said he wanted to get together," says Ellsberg. "So that was kind of doing my networking for me while I was sleeping, basically."

Social Proof for Social Media

Scott has regular conversations with people on Twitter. Twitter provides credibility; the header photo gives him the opportunity to quickly show he's legit. The bio allows him to quickly convey a lot about his business and other social proof. He can supply links to his personal website and his company. Last, he always keeps a pinned tweet to either something he has written on a key subject that defines him (like an article he wrote for Inc.com about being a master connector) or a major piece of press that offers third-party validation of who he is and what he's about. (In this case, it's currently an MSNBC interview he did about building community.)

"Why do I do all of this? Because I know the people I want to connect with are pinged all of the time, incredibly busy, and I want to make sure they connect with people who are aboveboard—and provide a valuable use of their time," he says. "Instantly, if I tweet to someone cold or get into an existing chat with my point of view, they can see who I am and what I'm about in five seconds. This helps break the ice digitally."

If Scott wants to engage in a deeper conversation, he'll ask to move to DM. Yes, he has many followers and verified status for additional social proof, but this first part is achievable by anyone. Even you.

Attracting an Engaged Tribe

Entrepreneur and angel investor Mark Suster started doing daily "Snapstorms"—short bursts of video around specific topics—that reach thousands of people. Each snap provides concentrated information that feels incredibly personal to each one of them.

Suster knows exactly what he is doing: Many of the people he wants to reach are entrepreneurs between ages twenty-one and thirty-five—the same age range, coincidentally, as Snapchat users. After noticing that most of his competitors, who are between thirty-five and fifty-five, tend to avoid the platform, he decided it made good business sense to embrace it. He doesn't care that the video goes bye-bye within twenty-four hours; he likes the "immediacy" and "authenticity" of it. He also likes the ability to reach so many people. As he says, "If I can help thousands with five minutes of my time daily? Why the fuck not?"

CHAPTER 9

THE DOS AND DON'TS OF INTRODUCTIONS

Novice connectors tend to go wild when they first learn to make introductions. Once they learn how to "connect the dots" and find mutual value, they jump at the chance to put it in action. This is a common mistake.

Our advice? Resist! When the time comes, there's a formula for just exactly how you're going to connect people, and the answer to the equation has many variables you have to first discover.

How to Make an Intro

A good introduction offers context, is matter-of-fact without being unnecessarily verbose, lays out the goals and mutual value—and explains how to accomplish all of this in either an in-person one-minute overview or a short email that actually gets read.

Basically, you're doing everything you can to ensure a successful introduction and experience for everyone involved before you ever make a single connection. Your job is to minimize risk, negative experience, and time sucks for people. Making sure they are fits and not forcing them.

Whether you're in the midst of an in-person conversation when you're both in the same room, or reaching out via email, you want to set the stage for the conversation in a similar fashion. It's all about building trust and putting your context and insights to work with others.

This introduction is giving you an opportunity for both sides to understand how thoughtful you are. That there is a *reason* you have put these people together.

How do you show how thoughtful you are? By demonstrating that you actually listened to them, that you helped them see who and what they *really* needed to be connected with to help them, that you were genuine in your intentions, and that you actually know what you're doing without having to market that "you're a connector," people will notice.

Other than the obvious—you're seeing the other person live instead of digitally—there are some subtle differences between online and in-person introductions. An email intro is planned, so you have time to craft a formal request. This should include a brief bio of each person, beginning with the recipient, the one who is getting the introduction.

You probably know what a terrible email looks like. It's the sort of missive with no context, no background, and no substance, that seemingly comes from nowhere: *"John, I met Jack at an event. You two should connect."*

THE DOS AND DON'TS OF INTRODUCTIONS

If you're not sure why this is useless, let us explain: It says nothing. Neither party has any idea why he should meet the other. Why should either one waste his time? What will he get out of it? What's the goal? (Not to mention the fact that people hate it and hate you for doing it.)

Now compare it to this:

Dear John,

It was great to meet you the other night at ABC event. Jack, CCd here, has even more insights about CMOs in the XYZ industry. Jack, John just launched his second business after a successful exit from the first one last year. He feels his new service will resonate well in the XYZ industry and has specific interest in learning more about what potential buyers in the XYZ industry look for when taking on new vendors. Given the success your business has seen in the XYZ industry for the past five years, I thought you'd be able to share some valuable insights with John.

John, Jack knows the XYZ industry very well as a former CEO in the space. I would also advise you to tell him more about your product because I believe there might also be some strategic synergies.

Please connect directly. Let me know how it goes.

The difference should be obvious, but in case it's not: In the latter example, both parties have a sense of who the other is, in stage and in stature. From the start, Jack knows that John is a relatively newer connection of the connector, since the connector said where he met John and that it was recent. The "why" of the introduction—that is, the ask and intent—is clear. And while the main ask is educational in nature, the connector uses his knowledge of John's product to allude to the fact that it might also be of additional value for Jack.

To recap: Be short and to the point. You shouldn't write a book, but you have got to give context for why the people are meeting. You need to articulate the premise—the who, what, when, where, and why. Where do the two parties intersect? How can this introduction benefit both parties' individual endeavors? What do you hope to accomplish as the result of their colliding?

Don't make assumptions and don't editorialize. Really good connectors can set up a conversation so the individuals in question can figure out for themselves why they should be meeting. When a connector is familiar with both parties, he or she can play a role in showing why the connection is valuable from all sides. So when we say don't editorialize or make assumptions, we mean that based on *not knowing* something versus *knowing something*. If you as a connector know something that will make the connection more special and valuable, offering a line or two is a good idea.

Take the example above. If the connector didn't know that Jack was looking for strategic alliances or that John's service wasn't a fit for Jack, the connector should not have included that he or she saw the potential for a strategic fit.

The same thing applies for in-person introductions, too. Here is a sample:

Bad: *John Smith knows everything about sales. He's one of the most awesome people I know!*

Notice that this gives no context, no rationale, and nothing for the person you are talking with to latch onto. Basically, there's nothing definitive that resonates.

Good: *John Smith is a chief revenue officer who has delivered consistent sales growth for his company in the Enterprise SaaS space for about ten years.*

This gives context, clarity, social proof through example, and industry, seniority, and track-record verification. In short, it gives a full picture of why this person might be the perfect fit for someone's needs.

Incidentally, good subject lines are equally important. A good subject line should contain both people's first and last names. This makes it easier for them to search for the message later on in a cluttered inbox.

Not long ago, Ryan tapped into his network to help a twenty-something friend in the early stages of his career find job opportunities in the SEO realm. He received tons of responses. But before making any connections, he had his young friend review all of the companies Ryan was going to suggest to make sure he thought they might be a reasonably good fit for him. He didn't want to waste either person's time with the possibility of an introduction that didn't have a reasonably high degree of a positive outcome.

Translation: You must always ask for more context as to why someone wants to connect. If you don't do this, you could be setting up an important contact of yours with a person who's trying to sell them something they don't want. Part of judging motivation and intent is not just conversation but also other factors, like the person's job or career ambitions. If they are a salesperson and their goal is to meet someone you know to try to sell them something, you need to think about whether this is an endeavor you want to participate in.

The Double Opt-In

One mistake new connectors make is ambushing someone. They're so eager to get started, they blindly reach out. This is a colossal no-no. Indeed, the very first rule of successful introduction making is something called the "Double Opt-In," a term coined by Adam Grant.

The Double Opt-In is exactly as it sounds: a connection between two people *who both agree to it*. Only in very select circumstances is it okay to make a blind introduction, and then only if you have such a strong level of confidence that the connection you're about to make is something both parties can't live without. (But that's Jedi-level connecting that you might not be ready for yet.) Otherwise, it is verboten. "If it's a high-level contact, I will have the person who wants the introduction write a few sentences, and I'll edit it down and pass it on, asking if it's okay," says Jon Levy.

David Cohen, the cofounder and co-CEO of Techstars, a worldwide network that helps entrepreneurs succeed, goes so far as to say that he will "connect anyone to anyone if it's a Double Opt-In. I know that some are higher-quality introductions than others. I try to understand the target and their preference."

A journalist we know came to us very upset over an email she had received. Someone she did not know well, whom she had talked to briefly on the phone months earlier, emailed her out of the blue. The sender wanted to connect her with a plastic surgeon who, presumably, wanted the journalist to write an article about her. This was not made clear, however. In fact, all the email said was, in effect, "You two are great. You have a lot to discuss—go for it!"

Our journalist friend thought the etiquette here was sorely lacking, and it was. It's not like the sender was a good friend of hers—they barely knew each other. Nor did the connector ask our friend if she had time to meet anyone or if she was in the mood to talk to anyone new. "I replied that I was busy and wished her luck with her project," our friend told us. "Was that okay?"

You bet it was! While there's no need to burn a bridge, you don't have to go out of your way for anyone, especially someone you don't know well. Had the person asked in advance, our journalist friend would have been much more amenable. Instead, the connector lost credibility, whether she knows it or not.

Every introduction should operate on a case-by-case basis, but you should always use your head. If it's someone you know well, you can just go for it. But if it's more nebulous, then you should be conscious of the person's time.

Obviously, if two people are in the same room, you have three choices: you can introduce them immediately, you can choose not to introduce them, or you can not mention it initially until you get confirmation in a private quick chat with the other person (a verbal opt-in, of sorts).

There are many more options to choose from in a digital environment, depending on the situation, the people involved, and your level of relationship with them.

When Is It Okay to Directly Introduce People?

With a direct email introduction, the connector has a strong enough relationship with the other party that he feels comfortable just reaching out. David Cohen frequently receives many requests for a specific person. In that instance, he'll simply write and say, "'I've been asked to make a lot of introductions. Do you want me to filter?' Most of the time I just forward and say, 'Would you like this?'"

However, you can get creative with your introductions. Jayson Gaignard is a huge fan of the Double Opt-In. In fact, he usually won't make any introductions without it.

Except when he does. Not long ago, Gaignard broke normal protocol when he sent a video introduction to Scott and to Derek Coburn, the author of *Networking Is Not Working*, whom Scott wanted to interview for this very book.

Rather than asking both guys if it was okay to introduce them, Gaignard shot a two-minute video intro and emailed it to Scott and Coburn. In the video, he listed both people's backgrounds and explained why he thought they should meet. "It was surprising and delightful, really," says Scott, who had never received a video intro before. "And the subsequent meeting went great."

Of course, the main reason this worked so well is because Gaignard knew both parties, their goals, personalities, and backgrounds, incredibly well. He knew the subsequent connection would be well received by both parties. It wasn't random.

If you feel confident that you are on good enough terms and they won't be offended by your doing a blind introduction, then go for it. But if you have any doubt, then you should go always go for the Double Opt-In.

Following Up

After making any connection, a good connector will reach out to both parties to see how it went. This doesn't require much—a quick email will suffice. You want to know what kind of value these people have gotten. If you really care about being a connector, then you want to have something to measure yourself against. You want to see what works, what didn't, and what you can do differently in the future. Also, you want to make sure it went as anticipated. If you find out that someone wasn't responsive or respectful of the doors you opened, it will help you to be more cautious when moving forward with that person.

Jayson Gaignard sets a reminder and follows up on every single connection he makes. For him, it's invaluable. It's important for him to see how it went, if it was good or bad, "and that I'm thinking the right way," he says.

When *Not* to Make an Introduction

Beyond knowing when to make a connection, a Superconnector knows when not to. Even if the person you're trying to help is really great, if you know it's a bad fit, don't do it. More often than not, *not* making an introduction is the right move. You can't give to everyone. Over time the quality will decrease. What you do for people will be considered added noise and not a welcome gift.

If you think of Superconnectors as educators or mentors who are looking out for the person making the intro request, then it's actually quite caring not to make the connection. "If you introduce someone who isn't ready, they will burn the contact and will be angry and disappointed in themselves," he says. "People have to be ready to manage communicating effectively with the people I introduce them to, or everyone looks bad."

Here are the six red flags for times when it's best to hold off:

1. When the goals of the person are not reasonable or rooted in reality. Or he or she is simply not ready.

A few years ago, a recent college graduate asked Jon Levy to give his application to the managing director of Techstars, New York. Levy asked to see the application. It was a disaster. "I told him straight out, 'I'm not going to do this right now,'" Levy recalls. "'Here's my feedback. You have to be prepared, and right now you are not.'"

Levy continues, "If I went in front of Richard Branson at twenty-two, I'd have embarrassed myself, and he would never have met with me. You have to let people develop a certain amount. I'm not going to send someone to the lions or in front of really important contacts unless I'm confident they have their shit together."

Levy was smart: He showed that he was genuine by refusing to make the connection. He also gave advice to the young person on how he should go about meeting people. And he also saved the person from likely having a door permanently closed on him.

2. When the intentions aren't authentic or the person seeking the introduction is a taker.

Some people will lie—either flat-out or by omission—to get what they are looking for. If you're unsure of their true intent, don't do it. You can't afford the risk. Again, this is your reputation, so you need to be very careful of whom you are associated with. You have to understand the chess pieces on the board, the rules of engagement. You will be defined by the people you introduce to others by the receiving party. If someone says, "I want to meet Z person in F industry" and they are a vice president of sales and it is obviously a sales pitch, the question is, is that a position you want to be in, helping to refer customers? It might be. It might also not.

"You have to be careful of people who want to break into your community," says Linda Rottenberg. "How they enter matters a lot. If they are just trying to hobnob with the most important people, it's just obvious and will rub people the wrong way."

3. When you are making assumptions or overpromising and the reality is that you likely can't make it happen and are going to look like a fool.

A lot of people make this mistake—"Bill Gates is my uncle's best friend, and I'm sure he'd love to invest in your new widget!" If this isn't true and you promise something impossible, then not only will you let the person down, but your reputation will also take a hit.

You also want to make sure to hold your cards and not overpromise anything to the initial party doing the ask. To that end, don't overextend yourself on nonguarantees. All you have are your bond and your ability. If you lose those, people will lose faith in your value. And the worst thing that can happen to a Superconnector is to not be seen as a worthy connector.

4. When the person they think they want to meet isn't the person they need to meet.

Some people are dead set on meeting a specific person for a very specific goal. No one else will suffice. Doesn't matter that this is absolutely the wrong person for them to talk to—especially since that person most likely wouldn't even be able to help them. Very gently let them know that you don't feel comfortable making the connection and explain why. Be honest—even at the risk of offending someone. This small moment of awkwardness is less painful than what *could* be if you were to go through with making a connection that's bad for the person you're connecting someone to because it's a waste of their time—or, worse, harmful to their business, bad for the person who requested the connection because they're investing in the *wrong* person to help them altogether, and bad for you because you bartered the connection and now lose credibility as a great connector of people.

A sample email:

Hey [INSERT NAME HERE], I'm always happy to make a connection. In this case, I actually think that this is not the right person for you to talk to, and I want to be respectful of your time and this person's. Instead, I recommend XYZ because. . . . I hope you understand. Let me know your thoughts, or give me more insight into why you think this is the right person to connect with and we'll go from there.

If the person continues to prod for the connection and you genuinely feel it's not a good fit, continue to be honest and don't be afraid to say no. The damage you could do to your reputation by not following your Superconnector instincts is far more important, and long lasting, than making this one person happy in the moment. In most cases, we've found that the frustration the other person might feel will fade quickly.

5. When you don't know the person they want to meet (either well or at all).

Sometimes a person seeks a connection with someone you really aren't that well acquainted with. In this case, it is perfectly fine to abstain in order to give the relationship more time to blossom.

Alternatively, you can be honest and let the intro seekers know that you're not the right person to make the connection. This happens to us quite a lot. Many people find us on LinkedIn, notice our connections, and think that we are best friends.

In truth, they're what we call a "vanity connection." That is, someone whom we connected with or they connected with us with little to no relationship building involved. Maybe the person read an article one of us wrote and reached out to us, thinking someday it might be of value. This happens all the time, and it's important to be honest when you're just not the right person. It's not a blow to your Superconnector credibility to just say no.

6. When it's a newer relationship of yours and you aren't sure that this is the first person you want to push their way.

There are times you might not know the right person but for whatever reason you don't feel comfortable sending this person to them. This is okay. Some asks are going to end up on the cutting-room floor—or never happen at all.

In other instances, you might not be the best person to make the introduction, either because you don't know the person in question well or because they're a newer relationship of yours or because you know the person likes connections a certain way from what you know or have heard and you aren't the right way in. Sometimes it might be best to connect someone to a closer connection to the end prospect you're seeking, as they have a better relationship (and the most important thing about an introduction in the eyes of the individuals being connected is their respect for the connector).

Now, what should you do if you make a connection between two people and it goes badly? How do you regain trust and repair that relationship? When is it worth preserving, and when do you have to move on? What kind of gestures and actions can you take to communicate that you're still of value to that person?

Technically, that shouldn't happen, because you have followed our advice up to this point. But things do fall through the cracks. So if two people meet through you and it goes badly, apologize. Let the person know that you feel terrible and that you did not expect it to go awry. Ask if there is anything you can do to repair the relationship—or, better yet, send a note or gift. Chances are, they will understand. They've probably been there before, too.

CHAPTER 10

THE COMMUNITY OF YOU

Who do you think is one of the most connected people in the town of Homestead, Florida, population sixty thousand? We'll give you a few hints. Over the past twenty-five years, he has held some variation of the following posts:

- chairman, treasurer, vice president, president of the Homestead Chamber of Commerce
- board member, treasurer, vice president, president of the Homestead Community Concert Association
- chairman, First National Bank of South Florida
- board member, treasurer of Homestead Rodeo Association (and grand marshal of the rodeo parade!)
- chairman, vice chair, treasurer of the Military Affairs Committee
- chair, Police Pension Board

- 2013 Citizen of the Year
- elder in two churches

Aha! you say. He must be the mayor. Or a billionaire. Or George Clooney. Or maybe a Kardashian cousin?

Nope, nope, nope, and are you *kidding*?

His name is Jim Pierce, and he is the local . . . accountant.

That's right: one of the most connected people in Homestead, Florida, is a sixty-six-year-old CPA, the guy people call in a panic in early April. Pierce owns one of a handful of small accounting firms in town, where he scours the tax returns of mom-and-pop businesses. He has built a long history of relationships that span generations, which have become consistent referrals over the years. "I know the mothers, grandmothers, and now the grandchildren, so it's a generational thing," he says.

Pierce didn't come out of the womb clutching a Rolodex. He didn't start off with money or connections—in fact, he didn't know a soul when he first moved to Homestead thirty-five years ago. But his goal was to set down roots there. Moreover, he never actively pursued any of the accolades, honors, or positions that have been bestowed upon him. Everything came to him organically. But come to him it did. Not by lighting candles and chanting some mantra, hoping the universe would bring people to him. But by carefully and selectively building a community around himself of the right people. By being consistent, by giving, by always looking to help the community. His methodology is easily replicable. You don't need to hold a swanky party atop a billion-dollar mountain; anyone can do this. Even you.

Pierce's journey to becoming one of the most influential people in his town started with one simple, and possibly most important, Superconnector talent: the art of community building. You can't go to school to learn how to be a master community builder (though we dream of a world where you could earn an Ivy League "community building" degree). You learn by first developing that thesis (remember, we talked about that earlier) and then going out into the world and putting it to good use.

We call this building the Community of You. That is, the people you surround yourself with that you've developed some semblance of relationship with that will ultimately help you do more good for others and ultimately earn ROI yourself.

There are many tactics for building community, and, as with everything in this book, there is no one-size-fits-all blueprint. We will talk about some of the strategies you might employ in this chapter, but only you can decide, with your ninja-like self-awareness, what paths are right for you.

The top Superconnector skill is being able to convene the right people around him- or herself, a.k.a. building their community. This can happen through assembling formalized groups, hosting events, creating online forums, and a plethora of other techniques. But before you jump into this headfirst, it's important to understand our definition of "community" in this book.

Defining "Community"

What Pierce realized—and what Superconnectors know—is that community building is at the heart of everything. He looked at all of his relationships and people in his community through his long-term lens. He knew he wanted to be a foundational part of the community where he lived and worked, and as a result that's how he built his relationships. Had he thought through the lens of "growing his business," he likely would not have been so successful in thinking about his relationships. The consistent long-term, nontransactional thinking is what enabled him to surround himself with the right people. And his consistency of giving to improve the place where he lives also attracted the right people who had similar intentions as him. It's how they not only create trusted connections but also maintain them. But Superconnectors have a unique take on the concept of "community."

Our definition is simple: *a collection of people who share some kind of commonality.*

Some communities cater to people in certain industries or from similar backgrounds. The idea is that people need to have some formal commonality in order for "community" to exist. This could be your professional status or job title (e.g., a group strictly for IT professionals or dog walkers). Or it might be something more comprehensive, like, say, that you're all entrepreneurs no matter what industry you come from (this is what YEC is). The value of this is enormous.

For our purposes, a "community" is composed of the people you surround yourself with, either purposefully or by sheer luck, whereas a "group" or "event" is the formalized structure, activity, or curation of people you associate with or bring together (more on that below). So YEC, for example, is a *group*, because it is formal and composed of select people from our greater community. Ditto for Adam Rifkin's 106 Miles or how

Jonathan Levy invites people to dinners or how David Hassell had his "Mansion Series."

A community is both something you can join and something already in existence, like, say, a family. It can be offline or online (or both). For deeper engagement, the best connectors put structures around some of their communities through formal activities like groups, events, or online communication channels (such as newsletters and forums).

The beautiful thing is that you can be a part of many communities—one for your town, one for your profession, one for your hobby, one for your family, and so on. Your community is always evolving and changing. It can be whatever you want it to be; it will grow and evolve as you continue to evolve and grow. You can continue to define and redefine the terms of it, in a way that works best for you.

Let's take physical location as an example. Even if you don't share the same political views with the people in your town, you all pay taxes and live in the same place. This makes you a community, because you all want to live in a stable and happy environment. You have a shared interest: the desire to see your town become the best it can possibly be. If you're not happy with your town, you can move (or do something to improve it). If you love it, you stay and maybe even double down on your commitment, actions, and effort. The people you surround yourself with are an important part of your life as well as a means by which others define who you are.

But Superconnectors know how to push the boundaries so they have a more vivid experience of community in all aspects of life. There are many reasons. For starters, communities provide a foundation for sharing knowledge with people who deeply care about the same topics and issues that you care about. They provide a way to get—and give—feedback, support, introductions, and referrals. Here are a few other benefits.

Access: The goal of any community is for it to naturally build itself and its value. A single person can add major value; dozens of individuals add infinite possibilities.

Imagine you want to meet the president of Coca-Cola. If we sent out an email today and tried to meet him, we probably could, but it would require cashing in on a few chits, opportunity cost, time, and a lot of our social capital. But when you know someone who has already built trust with the president—and they already trust you—you can cut time and energy. The value is obvious. So if you're in a solid, formed community with mutual value exchanged, you can leapfrog into the kinds of opportunities you're looking for.

Financial opportunities: We live in a "who you know" world. If you're a trustworthy and trusted individual, opportunities—business or otherwise—will naturally be sent your way. Doors will swing open that will allow you to create wealth and opportunity. You might not have consciously thought of it this way, but every opportunity to excel in your career and make more money was given to you because of relationships with other human beings. It doesn't matter if you're an independent entrepreneur or part of a larger corporate ecosystem: your opportunities are a by-product of your relationships, and as your relationships continue to blossom and develop depth, the more earning potential you will have in your life.

However—and this is important—if wealth is your main goal with a community, it will backfire. That is often the result of not being a meaningful participant or leader within a community.

Let's go back to Jim Pierce. Back when Pierce was first starting out, his mission was pretty straightforward: to be a responsible member of society. Not to make piles of money, not to be in public office, not to be a de facto mayor, but to be a good citizen. He knew he was going to plant roots and remain in Homestead for the rest of his life, and he wanted to play an active role there.

He knew that the right relationships would help him achieve his goal. So he went about building them. How did he do it? By following his purpose and never deviating from his original goals.

This doesn't mean he did not take opportunities when they landed in his lap. "One of my mentors said, 'You should be on the Chamber board,'" he says. "I knew it would eventually lead to business, but that wasn't the driving factor. The driving factor was to help the community, be involved, and do good things."

His attitude carried over into his personal relationships, too. Pierce befriended one of the other accountants in town, who had set up shop directly across the street from him. On the day he moved in, Pierce walked over and introduced himself. "I said, 'If you need anything or want to use the fax, you are welcome,'" he recalls. "You could tell by his body language that he was really standoffish and protective. He was very uncomfortable."

As Pierce made his way back to his office, it occurred to him that the young accountant was probably grappling with the same fears Pierce had dealt with at his age. He likely assumed that Pierce was probably trying to gauge the competition. So Pierce turned around and walked back over.

"You can't hurt me whatsoever," he told the new accountant. "You can't take any of my clients, and I don't want to take any of yours. You've got a good relationship with people who like you. So, I can't hurt you; you can't hurt me. In fact, if you need more clients, I'll send you some."

And that is exactly what he did. In fact, Pierce sent so many clients his way that the other guy actually asked him to hold off! They have an excellent relationship today.

He often thinks of an old adage he learned when he was younger: "Good friends don't make for good business, but good business makes for good friends."

Knowledge sharing and learning: If you're part of a small group in your local business community, sharing information can be comforting. You might be having a hard time during a specific quarter. But if you see it's happening to everyone, then you will understand it's not an isolated experience. This provides more context for you in conversation throughout your life.

Communities also create the opportunity to connect and learn about things that you know nothing at all about. This is one of our favorite things about YEC. We have entrepreneurs in every sector under the sun, from brick-and-mortars to high-tech startups. When the high-tech startup wants to start putting their product into a physical location, they have a friend on speed dial to help. And that brick-and-mortar, well, when they want to start offering some of their signature products to a wider audience online, who do you think they're going to call for e-commerce advice? You guessed it, the high-tech startup in the YEC family.

Who Should Be in Your Community?

You want the community you build to have depth. Meaning, if you want to be seen as a leader in the hospitality sector, you shouldn't just go out and make friends with every bartender in your city (although that's a great way to save money on cocktails). Instead, you want to tap into and build relationships within multiple subsectors inside the hospitality world: chefs, foodies, and restaurant owners; startups developing apps that support the hospitality world; and, yes, don't forget the bartenders, too.

You also need to know who you want to connect with when you have a very specific goal in mind. Say you're a fledgling startup in the Midwest and want to crank up your business to $1 million in annual revenue. You wouldn't just go out and ring the doorbell of every startup under the sun, would you?

No, you would not. (If you answered yes, we might need to have a little sit-down.) Instead, you would specifically seek out startups in a similar industry as yours, in the Midwest market, who have reached $1 million in annual revenue over the past year or two.

These specific focal points ensure that you home in on the right people who have actually solved the problem you need to solve, in a market similar to yours that they understand, in the same region of the country where some of the same hurdles may exist.

But building community is about more than simply gathering people together for a party. It's about carefully curating the *right* people to bring together. It's about—here's that word again—being *selective*.

Whether you like it or not, people judge you based on whom you pal around with. "You are defined by the people you surround yourself with," says Adam Rifkin. "Every single person should have some semblance of a community, but is that the community you want? Is this the only world you know?"

The idea is to remove all assumptions about whom you should be connecting with. In other words, the perceived or "obvious" network is not always the one you should be after. It's not always about meeting people in your industry and position or just meeting people who are potential sales targets. Those people, in fact, are so obvious that they've probably been hit up too many times, have similar offerings in place that they trust, or will wonder about your true intentions and back away. The *better* plan is to find nonobvious circles that can morph over time but start off serving a very specific, niche network that will be able to see real value.

What's the Point of Community?

If you're a small business on Main Street, then a community where members share data and insights might be the most valuable. But if you're talking about building something more aligned with a trusted adviser group, you might be better off targeting individuals who have previously sat on boards. So you must think about what you're building and what you're joining.

What is your goal for building a stronger sense of community around yourself? Career advancement? Okay, great. Except how do you define "career advancement"? And what specific role do you want? In what industry(s) are you thinking? How much money do you want to make? What kind of community is this going to be? Structured or unstructured? Formal or informal? Is it an invitation-only experience, or is it open to anyone? Who are the people you need around you so the community takes shape? And how and where do you meet them?

All of these questions, and hopefully some less generic ones that you architect yourself (be creative!), will help you come up with a *really* defined goal for your community-building efforts. From there, you can decide whom you need to meet. Ask yourself: *Is it someone who has the exact job I want in the right industry? Is it a direct decision maker who can get me that new career or (more likely) the people in their circles of influence who can make that all-powerful referral that eventually gets my foot in the door with said decision maker?*

CHAPTER 11

HOW TO FIND YOUR OWN COMMUNITY

No matter what your skill level, you need to work within pre-established groups or communities or through those that are associated with or that run such formal or informal groups in order to eventually build your own. Being a part of other people's groups—preestablished groups, meet-ups, professional organizations—before creating your own is smart, because you draw your anchors from them.

How to Curate Using Preexisting Real Estate

You enter groups and communities with the goal of further curating and finding the right people within them to be your anchors and others who make sense for the real estate you will then create in the future.

You should be an active and engaged participant within these communities in order to attract the kinds of people you want to meet and get to know better. But the goal needs to be to find the people who make the most sense to bring into your world based on the community you want to surround yourself with.

Connectors don't see the world the same way the rest of the world does. We speak differently. We make an impression differently. We use technology differently. And we control our surroundings differently. Superconnectors build value using preestablished networks, events, or groups to curate their own social capital and community.

Abby Binder, for example, runs Abby Windows in Milwaukee. She is also a member of several professional organizations, including the National Association of the Remodeling Industry, the Chamber of Commerce, and the Better Business Bureau; her company is a certified women-owned business. She has essentially built her business through these communities. "There's a huge value of professional organizations as you build your own business relationships," she says. "The access you get, the knowledge share, the idea that people are looking out for you."

Identify Your Anchors and Core Groups

YEC was very informal at first. Only successful entrepreneurs were allowed in, but there was no formal process or criteria, just selectivity to make sure we believed they were credible enough to speak to schools and the media—and eventually each other. But it was that selectivity and access that made for a special experience that everyone cared deeply about and respected and turned them into ambassadors and loyalists.

It wasn't until a year after its founding that we started charging for membership. We didn't do this, by the way, because we wanted to make money off people. The reason we wanted to turn it into a formal group was because we believed we could deliver much more value to those involved with a team and a budget. We realized that if we were going to have a formal membership organization, we would have to charge.

So how do you find these "anchors," the people with whom you build mutual value? That is, those folks you can trust to plant the seeds for your community's eventual growth?

Creating Your Own Formal Real Estate

Once you establish the kind of community around you, you'll often want to build even deeper relationships by building more structure in your community in the form of a group, event, or forum.

The best connectors take their informal networks and turn them into formalized communities through one of three mechanisms: groups, events, or online communication channels such as forums and newsletters. This is what we did with YEC and what David Spinks, the CEO of CMX Media, which organizes conferences, workshops, and professional training for community teams worldwide, does with his company's highly engaged Facebook group. It's what Jon Levy did by turning connections into dinners and salons.

Levy, if you recall, began by inviting a group of people to his house to cook dinner together. That was a formal event. He

then asked them to recommend other guests. Those people—
the ones who were recommended—went to dinner, and he
then asked them for referrals. And so on.

Jim Pierce is another example. Homestead, where he lives,
is a pretty rural area. Residents like to fish and hunt. So that's
how he builds formal groups: he amasses three to five hunting
enthusiasts for semiregular excursions. Hunting is a big part of
the culture where he lives, and he knew that doing that sort
of activity would be appreciated. Plus, it gives people a chance
to get to know each other in a different setting, doing something they all love.

In addition to hunting trips, though, he puts himself
around other family men because they tend to be well-rounded
professionals. "For some people, going to a local bar works
well," he says. "In this community, everyone hunts and fishes.
The good thing is that you are together for a good chunk of the
day, doing the same type of activities. It's not a casual time."

Create Meaningful Collisions

"Collision," as we like to call it, is key. We are not talking about
colliding in a smash-and-burn kind of way. We mean it as in,
quite literally, getting people to meet that might not otherwise
be connected. This involves a pretty strong vetting process in
advance to determine whom you want to invite.

Jon Levy invites people he knows and respects to his influencer dinners. He then has them refer other people he can invite to future events. Going in, everyone knows that they'll be
meeting some pretty incredible people. It's designed that way.

Jayson Gaignard, on the other hand, must personally know
you before he'll allow you to attend any of his events. There's

an application process, he conducts interviews, and he limits his event to 150 people, max.

These sorts of activities drive context, trust, and memorability.

Elliott Bisnow brings entrepreneurs, creative types, and celebrities together because he knows the collision of those individuals will create something special. He has held events on cruise ships and on top of the mountain he owns (yes, owns) in Eden, Utah. These events are all pretty fantastic.

Using Indirect Access to Establish Direct Relationships

Direct access: Scott built YEC, Scott met Ryan, and now they work together. Boom!

Indirect access provides value through association. It's like, "Well, I don't know Charlie, but we both belong to YEC, so we have that in common." There are both information and context. It doesn't matter if you don't know Charlie personally; you're both part of YEC—an organization that you both trust—and that is enough. The organization vouches for you.

The hope is that by gaining access to people indirectly, you will eventually be able to reach out to them *directly*.

This is why connectors like Adam Rifkin, Elliott Bisnow, David Hassell, and Jonathan Levy built formal groups or events. By doing so, they were building an engine that had the potential to attract exponential indirect access to thousands of other people. By doing this, they created indirect access to dozens or (eventually) hundreds or thousands of people whom they may not have invited to the group personally—*but other participants in the community did*. The community built itself around them, and they, as the center of influence, gain more indirect access to make direct relationships. This is how the best connectors build communities that take on a life of their own and benefit everyone involved, while simultaneously scaling their relationship-building efforts.

In our online YEC forums, we have had like-minded members connect by chance (serendipity!) and start new businesses together, buy or sell businesses to one another, form life-altering partnerships, and so forth.

That is what happened with Zain Hasan and Logan Lenz, two YEC members. In late 2015, Hasan, founder of National Insurance and HR Consulting Group (NICG), posted in the YEC members-only Facebook forum that he was seeking help managing his company's rapid growth. Logan Lenz, a serial entrepreneur, knew he could help. When they realized they both lived in Florida, they decided to meet in person.

Serendipitously, Lenz was already building a piece of technology around payroll company ADP's offering. The two men linked up; not long after, Lenz came on as COO and business partner. Together, they've brought NICG to the next level: a successful collision.

YEC is a direct part of the experience; we were responsible for the collision. So now we will forever be associated with it. This makes us happy. And proud.

CHAPTER 12

CREATING A REMARKABLE EXPERIENCE

Superconnectors don't just hold a party or meeting or gathering. They throw Happenings. Superconnectors are also unpredictable. Every so often, when you least expect it, they will surprise and delight you with something amazing: a much-coveted introduction, a ticket to a concert or sporting event, a thank-you note for a random act of kindness that someone provided to you. We call these things Remarkable Experiences, and they can be pretty much anything that's out of the ordinary.

We're not talking about bungee jumping from the Hoover Dam (although why not?). It could be a hunting trip with three or four buddies, as Jim Pierce does. It could be convening on a private mountain, like Elliott Bisnow and Summit. Or an intimate family-style dinner in a private New York apartment, à la Jon Levy. Or exclusive wine tastings courtesy of Derek Coburn.

Or it could be an exclusive party in a penthouse suite off the
Las Vegas Strip, as we have done with YEC.

Remarkable is a fluid term. It's about delivering the highest
level of wow factor to the people in your community. It's what
entrepreneur Darrah Brustein had in mind when she was building her organization, Network Under 40. Brustein noticed that
just about every "networking" event she attended felt cliquey,
awkward, and transactional. So she set the intention of throwing monthly "remarkable" events that were anything but.

To start, she had staffers (a.k.a. "ambassadors") wear
bright-colored T-shirts with the words *Let's Talk* emblazoned
on the back. That way "people can find them and use them
as their concierge or as a buoy to help make them feel really
comfortable," says Brustein. "These tiny little things that don't
necessarily feel that unique or high-tech really matter. On our
name tags we de-emphasize one's company and emphasize a
connection point instead, so you can find ways to help people establish kinship very quickly, like creating conversation
starters."

To foster conversation, at every event she and her staff
will ask a leading question that everyone must answer on their
name tag. "It really helps you get to know who someone is, not
necessarily just what they do," she says. "People are so much
more than that, and I think if you can honor that, people will
connect more deeply."

What she is doing is creating less friction so people can
focus on what you want them to do: meet people and build relationships. So if, for example, you're setting up a group dinner
where a check needs to be split, a remarkable experience would

be taking care of that ahead of time by creating a fixed price that everyone pays. As we all know, paying the bill with a group of people can be an awkward moment that sidelines authentic conversation. We've all been there. Brustein and company hold breakfasts and lunches called "Dine with 9," where they offer a flat-fee, fixed-menu pricing—which she picks up at the end.

Why Remarkable Experiences Matter to a Superconnector

Many of our own members have told us that YEC events have been some of the most life-changing experiences, but they most certainly did not start out that way.

When we were first starting out in 2011, we held a regular old event with zero forethought. We held it at one of our member's offices. We ordered lunch for all of the attendees and sat in a run-of-the-mill conference room together, but that's not the worst of it. When everyone sat down and started eating their lunch, the room fell silent. It was so awkward.

Ryan began by asking members to go around the room and introduce themselves, a relatively benign exercise. The only problem was that it took roughly five minutes for each person to tell their story. Thirty minutes in, people were starting to check their emails on their phones or blankly stare out the window and doze off.

To cut the tension, Ryan then asked members to talk about what they liked about YEC and what they thought we could do to improve the community. "In retrospect, it was so stupid," he says. "I made the conversation immediately about us rather than putting the focus on the members interacting with each other, having vulnerable moments, and solving real challenges together."

And oh yes? There were more staff than attendees.

After the event, Ryan decided to address the elephant in the room and queried some of our members about what went wrong.

In a word? Everything. Here's a (brief) summary.

- Members all knew each other or could have easily met each other. We didn't need to seat them at a conference room table with a bag lunch. They would have gotten more out of it by meeting new people outside of their regular Boston business circles.
- There was too much structure. We thought structure would be good, but it ended up making the entire experience flat. A more natural atmosphere where the right people could meet, relax, and chat would have been more appealing.
- It was flat-out boring. These types of meet-ups are a dime a dozen. Our members wanted something that was an experience. A few of them even mentioned that they'd have been happy to pay for it.

Depressing though it was, we appreciated the feedback. And it did force us to rethink everything from top to bottom. We fell into the trap of building an event that we ourselves likely wouldn't attend. And that's when we realized we weren't building anything memorable or remarkable. We were guilty of adding more noise.

If you don't believe us, just ask Morgan Brady, The Community Company's program director. She's an expert party thrower; she literally gets paid to create Remarkable Experiences. She clearly remembers that party:

> The thought of it still makes my stomach turn. We had a generous offer from one of our members to use a conference space in their office for a meet-up. "Awesome!" I thought and jumped at the opportunity. I didn't stop to think about the details, like that it was the middle of July and half of our members would be out of the office, on summer vacation. Or that maybe hot, heavy buffet-style Italian food would not be the most appetizing in the middle of summer or the easiest to eat at a crowded conference table. I also learned the hard way during that event that there is generally at least a 40 percent drop-off rate from RSVPs to attendance for a complimentary or free event. We ended up having more team members than guests, which just made everyone feel awkward.

She received a piece of feedback from that event that changed everything for The Community Company events. Matt Peters, the cofounder of Pandemic Labs and a longtime YEC Boston member and friend, told her that "networking for networking's sake is useless to me." "From that point on, all of our events have delivered an experience that is fully tailored to members of that community," she says.

So what does that mean, exactly? For Morgan,

> I do a lot of listening—in our forums to determine the common challenges people are facing, in all of our data points to discover where people are traveling, what types of events

they're asking for, conferences they are attending and even
median ages and relationship status, to figure out what types
of events make the most sense for most of our members, in
day-to-day conversations and on social media to learn about
what places and happenings people are excited about. Not
one decision is made without thinking of our members
first and how a particular element might be meaningful for
them. Ultimately, our in-person events and experiences are
thoughtfully curated to create an environment that is con-
ducive to conversation, connection—and a whole lot of fun.

Since then, we've upgraded the experience. We've taken
members everywhere from dive bars to some of the most
sought-after ski resorts in the world (and yes, they paid for it).
What made them so successful was the experience itself, which
led to organic conversation, which in turn led to serendipitous
opportunities for the people involved. We learned the hard way
that creating an exceptional experience took more than just an
evite and a reservation.

What we are all doing is building history, tradition, where
we see the same people event after event. Many of them have
become lifelong friends. People build exclusivity, demand, legacy, storytelling, natural word of mouth. That all creates great
value that will make you the center of influence on a very large
scale. But—and this is a big but!—it's not due to transactional
thinking. Rather, it's due to an experience crafted first and
foremost to build value for others, to create a setting where you
are able to be the chief giver and to build a world full of context
and trust.

Not everyone will do a private event at a conference or a dinner or go hunting. They might have their own experience in mind. Connectors find the real estate that works best for them. Sometimes it will be using other preexisting real estate to your advantage, like conferences. Sometimes it will be using circumstances and special occasions, as Jason Nazar, the founder of Docstoc and the CEO of Comparably, does. Nazar lives in LA, but he makes a point of seeing people in person as much as he can. He knows a lot of people, though—if he wanted, he could meet up with a different person every day of the year. When he comes to New York, rather than hold dozens of lunches with dozens of different people, he goes to a private room at the restaurant at the Standard Hotel, in the swanky Meatpacking District, and holds court there. Instead of bringing the mountain to him, he goes to the mountain. He gets to see everyone in one place, and they get to meet each other.

And once you build a strong enough community that's really sticky, it might become new real estate that isn't associated with anything else except the experience itself, like Elliott Bisnow's Summit on his private Powder Mountain.

The Step-by-Step Guide to Creating a Remarkable Experience

You know that adage "Don't sweat the small stuff"? Ignore it. "Sweating the small stuff" is what makes a successful Superconnector; Superconnectors sweat buckets about every last thing. Everything Superconnectors touch is meticulously thought out in advance. All the tiny details that feel random, spontaneous, and free-form? Those things may very well feel that way, but that's because someone behind the scenes has created this environment. Details, after all, are the key to success.

Superconnectors are notorious for behind-the-scenes magic. Nobody knows just how much planning, careful thought, and particular attention to details go into a YEC event. But because of the purpose and care that go into every element before, during, and after, we are able to turn an otherwise typical event into an Experience.

Just like a film, every experience has three phases: preproduction, production, and postproduction. It does not matter if you are hosting a conference, like we do, or simply messengering a new bathrobe. You still have to think about it before, during, and after.

Various elements make up each phase. If you follow these steps, we can pretty much guarantee that everyone—including you!—will have a spectacular, and productive, experience.

Phase 1: Preplan

For argument's sake, let's use a conference as an example. Conferences were originally designed to bring a group of people from all different regions together to network and share ideas around something they have in common. But as we hope we've shown, that model no longer works. There are so much work and noise at these big happenings, it's hard to find the true value.

That doesn't mean people don't attend them. They do, which is why new ones keep popping up faster than you can say "Javits Center." What this means is that conferences aren't going anywhere anytime soon. So why not use them to your advantage?

Many of our events take place at the same time as other large happenings, like SXSW in Austin, or the Computer Electronics Show (CES) in Vegas. We know that a lot of our YEC members will already be there, so it's a good time for us to connect in person. The other goal is to offer our YEC members something above and beyond what they're used to at a big conference. Something out of that mythical box. So we hold our events in more intimate settings, capping them at sixty people. But rather than meeting at the actual massive monster conference, we'll gather somewhere out of the way. We are actually providing a sense of relief.

People appreciate it. A few years ago, Scott was a keynote speaker at a conference in Cleveland, Ohio. It was held at a swanky hotel, with thousands of people paying big bucks to hear his words of wisdom. The other speakers were big-name investors and entrepreneurs as well, and Scott was looking forward to meeting them. It was the main reason he agreed to speak at the event, actually. There was just one issue: there was no event to get the speakers together! Nothing, not even a glass of V8. Scott was amazed. How could you not do anything for the speakers? Let's face it: speakers usually go to big events not just to hawk whatever product they have, but also to meet other speakers. But this didn't provide any opportunity at all.

So Scott being Scott (read: not shy, not afraid to speak his mind) approached the event organizer. "Do you mind if I put together a private, impromptu event for all the speakers?" he asked. He offered to lay out money for a small cocktail hour himself—he just needed the green light. The organizers were thrilled—it had never crossed their minds that the speakers might want something extra for themselves. "Go for it!" they said.

And what happened? Instead of a quick beer, the evening turned into a six-and-a-half-hour gabfest in a private room. All the speakers got to meet each other and speak openly and honestly. At the end of the conference, they all agreed that the speaker meet-and-greet had been a highlight. The organizers decided to make it a mainstay of all future conferences. And it only cost Scott a whopping $115 to build multiple close relationships and recruit several new YEC members.

The beautiful thing about holding an event while a preestablished happening is also taking place is that you're luring people who are already there. You are an *extra* perk. On top of that, you get the locals—that is, the people who live in the area year-round—so you're creating cross-geographical relationships that are highly valuable. In short, as curator in chief, you're selecting a handful of people who in your opinion *should* know each other and making it happen. This is not something that happens on its own. When you use preexisting real estate, you have so much more context to work with. Not only knowing where people are going to be, but also why they are there, since on social media many people often state their goals for attending or provide other valuable info that a Superconnector can extract.

You want to make sure that every single attendee will find your event or gathering different, worthwhile, and valuable. And you have to make sure that it doesn't inconvenience them—it enhances their experience or transcends it.

Of course, you don't have to rely on a conference to offer some kind of amazing experience. Another way of holding an event is the way Nazar does.

• **Identify your attendees.** When you are first getting started, you want to bring together anchors (and then other connectors) who will be key in spreading the word about your remarkable experiences—should they be successful and valuable, that is.

A large part, if not all, of what goes into phase 1 is research. Not everyone likes lists or spreadsheets, and you don't have to, either. If it's easier for you to keep track of things on Post-it notes, that's okay, too. The point is, you have to be organized because there are a lot of moving parts here. None of this is random. It might *feel* random to attendees, but it is all meticulously planned in advance.

Before any experience, we "research" every single attendee so we know who they are and what they do. Typically, we'll send out questionnaires in advance for them to fill out and send back to us before the event. What are they hoping to gain? What are they working on right now? What are they looking for? Is there anyone they want to meet? Is there a specific issue they are grappling with that they hope to resolve? We do a similar postmortem after our events, too (more on that in a bit).

We also let everyone know who else is going to attend prior to the event, just to give them some context. We send emails with each person's name, head shot, and LinkedIn profile, along with a fun fact about them (e.g., he was the seventh-grade bubble-gum champ in northern Virginia!). Superconnectors are a kind of concierge, acting as a liaison between each person and the rest of the group. For obvious reasons, this is a good place to be, because you are the key holder. You know all the players, and they know you. *You* are the common link. The entire event hinges on you.

We often use an app called GroupMe, which allows attendees to connect via an in-app chat a few days before an event. This is really helpful, especially if there are hundreds of people involved. This removes any pre-event friction, builds trust, and, again, puts context into the mix. By the time the actual event rolls around, people are already comfortable and familiar with each other. They've learned things about each other, and we've learned more about them. Even though we aren't responsible for every text or chat bubble, we remain at the center of influence for the overall network. Without sounding too touchy-feely, this builds congeniality and good cheer. And feeling—emotion—is what drives the best events or experiences.

Seating arrangements are something we also plan in advance. Whenever possible, we try to remove seating from our events. Nothing's worse than being stuck next to someone you don't want to talk to. However, in instances when we do hold seated events, we use the data we collected beforehand to put people who should know each other next to one another. Maybe they have a common interest or one is an expert in an area that the person next to him or her is trying to learn more about right now. Or two people might hit it off as potential partners based on synergies identified by our team. Then we don't tell them *why* they are sitting next to each other, other than the fact that they've been specifically placed there for a reason, so curiosity naturally sets in and conversation ensues (of course, if they can't figure it out, we tell them later, but even then that's a better way to find out because you've already had lengthy conversations with the other person).

Jason Nazar has combated this problem at his dinners by allowing people to stay in a seat for only fifteen minutes (or one course, max) before he requires them to switch tables. It's musical chairs, with a purpose: to talk to as many people as possible.

If we do have a seated affair, we always seat ourselves dead smack in the center, so we can see and hear all the conversations going on around us. Whenever possible, we avoid larger round tables and tables with more than eight people. This also allows us to contribute to each conversation—and, if necessary, introduce people to one another who haven't yet met. We're kind of like air-traffic controllers in this regard.

Phase 2: The Experience

As we have discussed, there are a million different kinds of remarkable experiences one can provide. You can go fishing. You can have a small dinner. You can spend an evening sampling every kind of bourbon known to man (or woman). Or you can gather together for a night of bingo. The actual event doesn't matter—it's not a one-size-fits-all kind of deal. You just want to make sure it's spectacular and remove as much friction from typical "meet-up encounters" as possible. The more unbuttoned-up you are and the more seamless everything feels, the more likely it will be that you'll have a successful outcome for everyone involved, including yourself. It's simple math: (good people + good environment + good context) - friction = Remarkable Experience.

As we've discussed earlier, we plan everything well in advance, down to the last detail. But to the attendees, everything feels natural and not regimented or too structured. Not only do each of our invitees know whom they'll be encountering at one of our events, but our team does, too. We train our staff to facilitate introductions among guests we know should meet. We make introductions right from the start, so that the second people arrive, they know whom they should talk to. They all appreciate it. They understand the value.

At most meet-ups, people spend the first thirty minutes trying to figure out whom to talk to or why they are there in the first place. We are trying to combat that. For most of our attendees, the goal is to meet the other people. By effectively doing it for them, we are making their lives easier. The ice has been broken—by us.

This helps us, too. By facilitating introductions for people on their behalf, it reinforces how well curated the event is. It's the Superconnector equivalent of a bottle of champagne and a Godiva sampler awaiting you at your hotel.

Beyond introductions, we also like to do other things that are unexpected, to create serendipity. You want to keep people on their toes, so that they feel that what they're experiencing is truly amazing. We've brought in a professional sommelier to some of our events or had people sample the best tequila in the world, educating them on the specific nuances. Elliott Bisnow offers speakers and activities at Summit. Bisnow brings in world-renowned thought leaders on a range of topics, many of which are truly out there—like shark tagging in the wild! Who thinks about shark tagging? People clamor to be a part of it. We encourage you to find your own way of doing things.

Take Jon Levy. He offers a structured framework where people can connect as *people* and not just as their job titles. One of his requirements is that all guests refrain from asking each other what they do for a living until the very end of the night. This way, people meet one another on equal footing, as people. Since everyone has a shared task—cooking—their bona fides don't really count. Doesn't matter if you are the CEO of Revlon or a clerk at CVS—you both have to brown the meat and fillet the chicken, thus creating an even playing field. Levy's events bring people down to their most essential element: as people. He eradicates any fears that may arise from people's own insecurities about their position in life.

As a connector, that's your job: to circumvent the bullshit. To bring people back to their essential selves.

Remember: The Superconnector is not a participant! We are merely facilitators—background scenery at best. Many people try to turn everything back to themselves, but that's exactly what a connector should *not* do, especially not at their own event. Experiences mustn't become transactional for you as a connector. That destroys the authenticity your experience stands for and will likely have a negative impact against you later on.

At Elliott Bisnow's Summit, he and his team serve the food to all of the guests. Bisnow himself ladles and spoons and carries dishes and plates back to the kitchen. It's a nice gesture, a show of humility, and part of the experience. And also—ding! It's a way to interact with every single person in the room. What better way to meet people than handing them a kale-in-a-blanket?

"We want that campfire feel," says Bisnow. "We just want to give it a really authentic communal feel. Also, it makes it feel like a family dinner party. It doesn't feel good when you're just up on a perch and people are serving you. We feel like we are part of the community, and it's a surreal thing: the team offering the event will also serve you the food!" (In return, they ask all guests to bus their own plates.)

At our annual conference-like event held at a ski resort in Utah for YEC members (no spouses or kids allowed), Scott went from person to person with a bottle of bourbon in hand, proffering conversation and drink. He met every single person this way—and, lest you wonder, he did not end the evening in a drunken stupor. (You can sip judiciously, and no one has to know otherwise.)

These kinds of meetings foster genuine, honest communication, "the kind of conversation people never have in the press," says Scott. "If you're dealing with sexism in the workforce or bankruptcy, it's the first thing you wish other people would say. Then you realize a Remarkable Experience doesn't need to be remarkable in a sense of what it does. It's about the context and the relationships involved and the circle of trust you've built around the experience that enables vulnerability to inspire real conversation."

At our events, we help people share the areas in which they are experts. At many "networking" events, people are supposed to go around the room introducing themselves. Usually, the facilitator says something cute, like, "Don't talk too long!" Everyone laughs, and then people drone on and on and on. Giant snoozefest.

To combat that, we limit everyone at our events to thirty seconds. We ask you to tell us your name, your company, one thing you need help with, and your area of expertise. Boom. That's it. Direct, to the point—it conveys all the pertinent information and delivers context to everyone else in the room that they can apply to their own situation. It doesn't need to feel like a full bio reading or like a bar-mitzvah boy at the Torah.

See, a Superconnector's job is to amplify context. We know that most people can't ask questions of other people. We know that people are bad at talking about things that are important to them. We remain at the center of influence, and everyone else becomes more valuable to one another. A win-win across the board.

Scott also tends to brag for someone after their intro. They can say the smaller details, but then he can take it over the top *on their behalf.* So if something amazing just happened, he can broadcast it. "When it comes from me, it's validating and appropriate," he says. "Shows I listened. Makes the person feel great. And gives everyone in the room more context. I'll say, 'John just sold his company for a lot of money' or 'Sally just raised a Series B' or 'Mark just had a big feature written on his biz in the *New York Times* that you should check out.'" Of course, he knows all of this because he's studied up on the person or had contextual conversations leading up to this part of the evening that he can then use to promote people.

The other thing that works about Bisnow's, Levy's, and our events is that they are consistent. Levy's dinners take place every month in different cities. Summit happens weekly in different seasons, with large experiences annually. And our members know that our YEC Escape, a three-day event in Eden, Utah, is held every year over Super Bowl weekend. Consistency builds tradition, natural storytelling, and affinity, and, longer term, nostalgia leads directly to promotion and referral.

At our events, we rarely if ever conduct or speak about business. The only time we do is if a member comes to us with an idea of how we might work together in the future, but even in that situation we respectfully say we will find time after the experience to follow up and talk more. The logic is simple: if their experience is stellar, there is a much higher likelihood for a successful partnership or business relationship to develop.

Phase 3: Postexperience

Most event organizers fail because they think their responsibilities end when the experience is over. But that is exactly what *not* to do. And this applies to a conference, a thank-you note, a gift—anything.

Our job continues after the doors close and we wave goodbye. Because now is the time to make sure we follow up to ensure people met everyone they needed to or that we felt they needed to and also to see what worked and didn't so we can add to our formula.

After all YEC events, we follow up with participants, sending them another email with a series of questions: Did you get to meet everyone you wanted to? If not, can we make the intro now? Is there anything else you need to know? Any information about the next event? Can we help you with anything else?

We also want to know what was valuable—and what we could have done better. What worked? What didn't? After hearing their conversations and the context we provided, where applicable we offer additional support or connections to resources or people that weren't present at the event.

We also typically send out a list of all attendees afterward, so everyone can keep track of one another.

The experience does not end with "Good night." Instead, it continues with your being seen as the center of influence and ensuring that each guest got the most bang for his or her buck.

CHAPTER 13

KEEPING IT ALL TOGETHER

All of the Superconnectors in this book have at least one thing in common: they are amazingly disciplined and consistent. They each have various ways and systems for maintaining their relationships. Though they all use different platforms, it's a habit for all of them. They systemize, build, and maintain regularly, every day, religiously.

Part of a Superconnector's mystique is that no one really knows how we do the things we do. You know how East London boy Steve Sims manages to meet people and frolic with CEOs, studio heads, and heads of state. But you *don't* know how he stays top of mind and manages to maintain these relationships.

This is a good thing! It's ideal, in fact. Audiences don't need to see the endless rehearsals that went into *Hamilton*; they just need to see a perfectly executed Broadway show. The same thing goes for Superconnectors. No one has to know how the secret sauce gets made. All they need to know is that the sauce

is in front of them, and it tastes amazing, and all the other pa-
trons keep clamoring for more.

In this chapter, we'll show you how we keep all the information together. We will explain how we organize all of our
information and all of our contacts. But don't tell anyone else.
It's our secret. Ssssh.

Rethinking How to Use Technology

Technology has done many wonderful things for the world. It
has allowed us to connect faster and farther, reaching people in
far-flung places whom we might otherwise not have access to
(e.g., CEO bigwigs on Twitter). But it isn't supposed to remove
real-life interactions altogether. The problem is that we've let
it supplant just about everything meaningful in life. Not even
The Jetsons did that! Technology is meant to be an *enhance-
ment*. You're never going to be able to replace a profound relationship with your Twitter feed.

The way we see it, technology should *add*, not remove, humanity to your life, business, and processes. In everything you
do, you want to determine the best way to convey your humanity, not de-emphasize it. To show care and value and not to
turn communication into a quick one-off, self-promotion, or
thoughtless emoji spew.

However—and this is important—some of our most valuable business relationships began online and remain largely
digital *to this day*. There are some people in our network we
have never met in person. Still, they provide tremendous
value to us, and each other, and we think of them as trusted
connections.

What really matters is not which tool you use, but how you use said tool. The content, context, curation, and connectivity. For example, using an email Listserv as a communication mechanism might seem really unhip, but if that's the platform of choice for the audience you're connecting to, then that's the platform you should use.

In each instance along the way, profit motive and marketers bastardized formats from Facebook to LinkedIn to email communication, and most people turned off. Instead of using these technologies to continue conversations and community-building efforts, we turned on the marketing and wanted to find ways to use all of the new stuff instead of just improving upon the original intent. Even crazier, most people who use these tactics, like a mass email blast to their Rolodexes, if you were to ask them "Do you read stuff like this?" or "Does this type of thing engage you?" would say no.

Most, if not all, of us promote and partake in activities that we don't believe in because many of us have fallen victim to the "that's the way to do it" mentality. Yet if we were on the receiving end, we wouldn't do it. Therein lies the conundrum we need to break—and this logic follows suit on every platform.

Connectors think about technology differently from the masses—specifically, in five different ways. Connectors use technology to engage, research, convene, enhance, and organize. They do not, however, use it as an advertising tool or self-promotional platform (to try to draw people to come to you through mass-marketing techniques) or to build deep relationships. You can create valuable relationships online, some of which may stay dominantly, if not totally, digital. But it requires

you to think differently about how you use technology—
to go beyond the surface level of what most people present
about themselves online and offer something more vulnerable
about yourself for them to connect with. Let's break each one
down.

Engage: This is the ability to attract someone's attention. To be
successful, authenticity and a lack of surface-level BS are key.
From there, real relationships can be formed; whether they stay
online or transform into something else is completely up to you
and the new connection you have made. This is especially powerful for introverts.

David Spinks, the CEO of CMX Media, relies heavily on
Twitter. "I joined Twitter in its early days; it became an invaluable networking tool throughout my career," he says. "It's an
equalizer. I was nineteen years old, and I'd follow these big-
name CEOs and read their blogs. I'd then respond to them on
Twitter, asking a question or challenging a statement, and start
a thoughtful conversation. They had no idea how young or un-
important I was. They'd respond, and I'd get to connect with
people I had no business interacting with."

Spinks does not use Twitter for entertainment purposes;
he's not gunning for a membership in the Friars Club. "I use it
to get information, as a way to connect with people I respect,"
he says. "I use it to build community."

Ditto for Facebook groups. His company's CMX Hub group
on Facebook has become one of the top online destinations in
the world for community builders to convene, share knowledge,
and exchange valuable resources with one another.

Research: Technology enables you to better identify those you wish to know or gather more context about those individuals you will be meeting with in the near term (people you know well for updates or those you haven't met yet). Social media also allows you to see the daily context that the people you want to meet are sharing with the world. In a world where so much info is out there on people and the businesses they're a part of, there's no reason to not know the basics before you sit down with someone. And for the stuff you can't find, have questions prepared that you want to have answered.

You might think that Googling someone before you meet them for the first time is a bit stalkerish. But it actually shows that you've done your homework before a meeting. LinkedIn is always a great place to start in terms of getting background on someone, but we also like to look at the "News" section of search results to see if they've been recently picked up by any press outlets or have a column of their own someplace reputable. The intel we gain doing this quick exercise gives us more to talk about when we meet in person.

Besides, everyone—literally everyone—does it. According to BrandYourself, an online reputation-management company, 1 billion names are Googled every day. And 75 percent of human resource departments are *required* to research a candidate online before making a hire. And guess what? Seventy percent of them have rejected candidates based on information they found online, while 85 percent say positive information has influenced them to make a hire. In other words, your reputation matters. A lot.

Convene: Bring together different segments of your network or communities for thoughtful knowledge sharing and value exchange.

As we mentioned above, Spinks has created the most robust networking group for knowledge exchange in his industry (community professionals), and it all started for free using little more than a Facebook group. Now it's a full-fledged business with several revenue models, including training, consulting, research, and events, working with some of the world's largest companies. (The CMX Hub group on Facebook has more than six thousand members and is drawing in hundreds more every month.)

Enhance: Once the foundation is set, you are able to keep in better touch with those with who you are already close to enhance your relationship over time.

Steve Sims, the CEO of The Bluefish, uses text and email to reach out to people, and he often uses video text, where he takes a video, records it, and sends it on. "You get my energy, my voice," he explains. "Recording the videos for me is far faster than typing, yet it contains so many points of communication—tone, style, passion, what mood I'm in. I could be in a dungeon and take a video: 'Hey, we haven't talked in a while, and I thought of you . . . ' "

Not long ago, Sims, an avid motorcyclist, received a new racing suit. Designer John Blas—the man who designed and drew the "beast" from Disney's *Beauty and the Beast*—had done an emblem of Sims's face on the suit. The two men hadn't seen each other in person for years. So Sims finally did something about that. "I had a glass of whiskey in my race suit in my living room, and I quickly recorded it and texted him," he recalls. "I don't owe him anything, but you never know in the future what's going to happen."

Indeed, this was a good move, because it provided a perfect reason for Sims and the designer to be in touch. So you might want to make a list of the people you want to check in with or those whose radar you want to remain on—and then, of course, do it.

Organize: Ever heard the phrase "Work smarter, not harder"? Tribes of life-hacking enthusiasts live by it, and the philosophy can apply to how you manage your relationships, too. A CRM is just one example of a specific type of technology that can help you do this, but it doesn't have to be a top-of-the-class, bells-and-whistles-packed system like, say, Salesforce to be effective. It can be a middle-of-the-road, highly affordable product like Contactually, which Derek Coburn uses.

The options are limitless, and a CRM is only one way to build community. For example, you can use a tool called Boomerang, like our friend Jayson Gaignard, to have Gmail remind you when to follow up with someone. Or else you could use a similar plugin called Mixmax to put Gmail on steroids. Our pal Jared Kleinert swears by it.

Ryan Bethea, a sales and marketing executive, has a novel way of organizing his contacts. In addition to the standard filters, he likes to tag people based on how they can best help others. "It makes it infinitely easier to get people connected to what they are looking for," he says.

While tagging people by industry is great, Bethea feels that this system also helps cut through the "snap-judgment" culture we have built. "People's titles don't tell the full story at all," he says. For example, Bethea knew a financial adviser whose clients happened to be professional athletes. "Tagging him just under 'Finance' wouldn't really do him justice," says Bethea. (He filed him under "Sports.")

CHAPTER 14

STAYING ON TOP OF YOUR NETWORK

To the outside world, staying on top of your network looks natural and effortless. And many people assume they need expensive—or, even worse, custom built!—software or tools to do so. Or they need the things with every bell and whistle. Nothing could be further from the truth. This is an exercise in simplicity. Get-it-done-fast tools are better than get-everything-you-can-think-of tools by far. People tend to get distracted by shiny pretty objects and try to get use or go off script in bad ways. You need to master basics. Set up the right frameworks to train yourself.

And remember: there is no perfect tool or "right" way to handle this. Whatever works for you is the way to go. Experiment with different tools until you find the one that makes it easy to do what you do best.

The best Superconnectors have created templates so that on the "spur of the moment," they can connect with people in their network, with just a few pushes of a button.

"Accessible connectors are organized," says Ryan Matzner, cofounder of Fueled, an app-strategy design and development firm in New York and cofounder of Sloane's List, a seven-thousand-member, invitation-only Facebook group for posting job openings and résumés. "They have to be if they're going to be a connector in the first place. Because they have to have some system, whether it's mental or formal, to make those connections. And so at a certain point, as the volume increases, they start to productize in a sense. Anything from 'All right, I'm just going to create a Facebook group, or a newsletter, or some way to bring efficiency to the system,' just like they would any other aspect of their life or business."

Matzner, it should be known, was *not* the most organized individual. That is how he came up with Sloane's List in the first place. He and his cofounder, Courtney Boyd Myers, were receiving email requests from people in their network who were looking for jobs or looking to hire.

"I'm always really happy to help any of those people, but I'm generally not able to because I'm not good at creating a mental database of all of these wants and needs," says Matzner. "Essentially I would need to be a market maker of 'Okay, yeah, you're looking for a job in marketing. Cool. Three months ago someone asked about that.' And I was describing this frustration to Courtney, and she mentioned the same thing."

They eventually created Sloane's List as a place to put all the requests they were getting. (Sloane was the name of a girl he was dating who had lost her job and was looking for new employment.) "It was a way to build a tool that would solve a problem," he says. "In the very beginning, it was just me and Courtney taking all those things we received, pasting them ourselves. And then as people started to ask us for favors, we'd reply back, 'Actually, I've built something that should help with your problem. I've invited you on Facebook. Here's a link. Go ahead and post.'"

Adam Rifkin created his "Five-Minute Favors" to keep himself accountable and make himself an effective giver. But again—there's no magic behind it. It's *consistency*. Eventually, if you do something long enough, it becomes second nature and you do it without thinking about it.

Bucketizing Your Community

Staying top of mind—that is, remaining relevant—is a Superconnector's bread and butter. If someone has a problem that needs solving, you want to be the first person they call. At YEC, if someone is struggling with, say, a personnel issue, we want them to say, "Oh, let me talk to Scott or Ryan!" When that has occurred, it means you've become a part of that person's utility belt. You're the go-to person. The person they absolutely must reach out to before making a move. This is an excellent position to be in.

Now, if you're a Superconnector, you know hundreds (if not thousands) of people. Keeping track of them all can be challenging.

One of the first things you have to figure out is how to categorize your contacts. For instance, do you have a bucket for tech people or for chief executives who earn over a certain amount? Creating a grid system of where people belong helps you privately keep track of different social spheres and other influential areas you are a part of. Segmentation helps you deepen relationships and build context around them.

Michael Roderick, the founder of Small Pond Enterprises, a consultancy for entrepreneurs, was a high school English teacher who then became a Broadway producer. He estimates that when he made the transition, he took close to two thousand one-on-one meetings, talking to people from as many different industries as possible.

To keep everything all straight, he uses . . . a spreadsheet. Yes. Really. "I have a spreadsheet of the people that I've made introductions for and who I really feel are just solid people, and I have notes in the spreadsheet of what they do and what types of things they're looking for, all sorts of different factors," says Roderick. "So whenever somebody comes to me and says that they need something, I search that spreadsheet. I actually do a search on the spreadsheet for the keywords and find people who fit those categories. It makes it pretty easy to find folks and be able to connect them and sort of help them with that particular process."

He has a system in place, but it's not what you might think. In addition to all the regular stuff—the person's name, where they met, what they discussed—Roderick also has a "Notes" column where he includes all the things most people do *not* talk about from a professional standpoint. "I'll have a 'Notes' column that says things like 'Cousin worked for Teach for America' or just little things that are brought up that are important for different individuals," he says. "It gives me that ability, if somebody mentions something, to be able to just search it and find it. So that column is one of my most powerful, definitely."

He has also created a grading system, what he dubs his "ABCD system" (you can take the guy out of the classroom . . .).

A's are the Advocates, the people who tend to be much more focused on helping and supporting you.

B's are the Boomerangs, "the people who are a little more transactional, a little more networky," he says.

C's are the Celebrities—people who have a team, some certain level of notoriety, and would be helpful to somebody else in another circle.

D's are the Drains, the people who, at this point in their life, "have more need than things that they are willing to contribute."

"When I put that down, I can start to filter by those ABCD categories and see how long it has been since I last talked to my Advocates, because these are the people who usually don't advocate for themselves," he says. "They're usually the ones who never ask me for anything, so it's really important for me to go to them and say, 'How are things going? What do you need?' because they usually will not tell me. So I have to sort of stay on top of those people."

He devised this plan, by the way, after realizing that each one of those two thousand meetings fell into three categories. The first was what he called a "steamroller meeting," in which the other person spent the entire meeting pitching him on whatever their service or product was.

The second type was the "two-way-pitch meeting." "They would ask me what I did. They would ask me about good referrals. They would tell me what they did. They would say what they thought are good referrals. And we never really got into anything else."

The last group was what he called "great conversations." They did not talk only about professional activities, but he enjoyed the conversations. "When I was having these great conversations, they tended to be much more engaged and interested in what I had to say and willing to help and willing to support in different areas," he says.

After realizing that, he decided he could take each meeting type and assign a specific character—an archetype—to each of these people. "Once you notice patterns, you can start to develop frameworks and archetypes for yourself and make life just a heck of a lot easier," he says.

Again, this is a guideline and one way to think about segmenting, but it's not the gospel. Your system needs to work for you, but key insights are to ensure the data are easily accessible by you on any device, instantly searchable, and highly organized in such a way that you can readily use your shorthand searches and codes to get what you need.

Time Management

Beyond being amazingly organized, Roderick is an excellent time manager. But the best connectors are. They make time to help other people—they are more than happy to do so— but they also take time out for themselves. When you become a connector at big-league levels, more people are going to be clamoring for your attention. You don't want to be rude, of course, but you also don't want to spend time on people who don't have a formulated ask or who you might think are less than awesome.

Adam Grant has thought long and hard about this. To him, being a connector requires being thoughtful about who you help, how you help, and *when* you help. "What we see with failed givers is that they try to help all the people all the time with all the requests, and they end up sacrificing their own success, as they devote so much time and energy to helping others that they fall behind on their own work," says Grant. "They get exploited by more selfish takers, and they end up contributing in ways that are actually not all that effective."

Successful givers, however, recognize their limitations. They know that they cannot help everyone equally. It's about being—yes—*selective* in whom you help and how much you help them. "It's about blocking time on your calendar to get your own work done and saying, 'Look, you know, I have windows where I need to progress toward my own goals,'" says Grant. "Yes, I will set aside time to be helpful to others, but I'm going to try to manage that so that I haven't given away my entire calendar, you know, for ad hoc requests."

Derek Coburn has more than twenty-five email templates saying no to different requests. He's not being a jerk—he wants to be helpful. But he wants to make sure he is the right guy for the job:

> I don't have time at all to meet or talk with anybody unless
> I know why we're going to be talking and if I can add value

for them and/or vice versa. Before I had these templates, I would get emails like, "Hey, can you be a guest on my podcast? Can you write a guest blog for my website? Can I pick your brain?" Sometimes, especially if I knew who the person was, I never looked forward to typing that email. It was like, okay, what do I want to say? How can I be nice about it?

So a handful of the templates will say, "Thanks for reaching out. I am currently focused on a few key priorities right now and more than likely don't have the time to allocate. In the event I may still be able to be helpful, can you let me know if there's anything in particular you were looking to discuss or wanted my feedback on?" Nearly 75 percent of the time he doesn't even get a response!

"Those people don't even know what they want. They just have enough free time on their hands that they want to meet people," he says. "I know I'm responding in a way that is true to who I want to be and with a reply that is consistent with how I want to reply."

We often joke that the most important people in our professional lives are Stephanie and Kiri, our priceless assistants, who know more about our whereabouts on a day-to-day basis than our families do. They know when we are free to talk and when we are not. (We both have certain days or times when we are simply not available.) They both know how to schedule meetings for us in every type of circumstance; they know the cafés we go to, so we don't have to travel across town to meet someone. How long should a coffee take? Thirty minutes? An hour? We both have our own preferences. For example, Scott limits most calls to fifteen minutes. "If it can't be completed in fifteen minutes, then we should be meeting in person," he says.

Even more important: our assistants know when to make an exception to our rule. They are trained to know that if someone is a big name or CEO or influencer, then we are more than happy to go on their turf. If this is a person we have been trying to meet, then damn! We will travel anywhere to accomplish this goal.

Jason Dorsey, the president of the Center for Generational Kinetics, a millennial and Gen Z research, speaking, and consulting firm, also meets people where they want. Invariably, there are generational differences. "To some generations, it might mean, 'Let's meet for coffee'; for others, it might mean, 'Let's set up a phone call or Skype call or Google Hangout,'" he says. "The trick for those who want to build meaningful relationships is to see your own biases or patterns for how you are used to making new friends and be open to changing those patterns to meet new people." In other words, if you prefer LinkedIn, or going to a social mixer, or attending a conference with executives, that's your bias. Once you're aware of it, you can intentionally choose to mix it up so you meet new people in new places.

It's to your benefit to adapt to people's preferences. "People who adapt to the person they want to engage with are often more successful in getting meetings and building new relationships because it's less stressful for the person you want to meet," he says. "Every relationship takes on its own dynamic once it's begun, but the more difficult you make it for the person in the beginning, then the harder it's going to be to have a chance to build a relationship with them long-term."

Dorsey acknowledges that this can initially be uncomfortable for people of any generation who are conditioned to engage with others in a certain way (e.g., by text or Snapchat). But those who are flexible are the ones who create the greatest likelihood to build diverse friendships that open doors and make the world more meaningful.

Setting Up and Maintaining Formalized Groups

Just as you've set up a framework for how to segment your networks, you also need a framework for how you will manage and create formalized groups or experiences.

First you need to determine the group's bylaws. Are you going to have written rules that are clearly stated, or are there more amorphous situations where the rules are simply implied? Are you running a Facebook forum with specific rules to participate, like Sloane's List? Is it a dinner with a referral-only policy on attendees, like Jonathan Levy's dinners? Or is it more of a member community, like YEC, that has guidelines and policies for both events and online discussions?

Clear-Cut Clarity and Rules

You must clearly spell out what the rules are in your organization. With some groups—say, Summit—members are not allowed to post anything on social media when they are attending certain events or in particular locations during Summit experiences.

In YEC we have an informal "no asshole" rule in place. (Well, actually, it is formal; we just don't put it in writing.)

We're joking—kinda—but you have to think about these things. Obviously, the word *asshole* is subjective; one person's asshole is another person's savior. We think of it like porn: you know it when you see it.

In the Superconnector world, assholes are pretty easy to identify. They are usually those folks who are clearly out for themselves. You know whom we're talking about: the sorts of people who take, take, take, who are the opposite of team players. The sorts of people who are quick to ask you for help but reluctant to reciprocate in kind. You know: assholes.

The good news is that assholes don't have a long shelf life. The even better news is that we have been successful at policing our community precisely because we *don't* have to police it. Community members tell us what the line is (i.e., you're an asshole!). If you have a solid group there for the right spirit and intention and multiple people are saying, "This crosses the line," then take note: it crosses the line!

Having said that, the best communities are those that make rules and *follow* them. You have to enforce rules and be clear. What are the rules of engagement? What do you want your community to stand for publicly? When people talk about your network, what do you want them to say? For example, when they talk about YEC, they usually say that we are "the most influential youth entrepreneurship organization in the country." We like this.

In most groups we create with our partners through The Community Company, we disapprove of anything overly promotional in nature. That could mean blog posts members have written, deals or discounts their companies are offering, links to donate to a charity they're supporting, and so forth. It's not that we think these things aren't necessarily valuable in the right environment. They're just not right for our groups, which people join to get away from the noise that makes their social media experience less valuable.

We shy away from anything that can cause members to get vicious with one another. Politics is a no-no in The Community Company groups. So is talking smack on vendors. If you had a bad experience with a vendor, our groups are not the place to vent. Why? Because in the well-connected communities of people we curate, someone inevitably knows someone at said company (or actually might work there themselves), which can lead to a not so exceptional experience. And keep in mind, we used the phrase *talking smack* and not *asking for help*. Often, members come to our support groups with an issue with a vendor, someone has a connection there, and problems get solved. Obviously, it's not always easy to be black and white—there will often be a couple of gray areas that can't be avoided, and that's okay.

Enforcing the Rules

How do you make sure people follow rules? Making them known from day one is a good jumping-off point. One way to do this would be to send a personal welcome message to your newest group members the minute they join. Be *very* clear about what the rules are. At The Community Company, we send new members a detailed document with all the guidelines. Inevitably, people will break the rules anyway, and you'll have to step in and remind them what they're doing doesn't fly. But if you set up the ground rules early, they won't be able to say "Oh, I didn't know!" and you'll have more of a case for deleting their posts than if you didn't properly communicate from the get-go.

Sloane's List has rules that members must adhere to. But while they are seriously enforced, they're nothing too elaborate. It's mostly about remaining consistent and having protocols in place to keep everything aboveboard when things go astray.

When Ryan Matzner and Courtney Boyd Myers were creating Sloane's List, they initially chose to let people in who were part of the "small to medium-size" circles around them. "It was people who we knew would get it and would post the right jobs and not post the wrong ones," says Matzner. "And then we gave everyone in the network the power to invite people in their network. And each invitation is then queued up for approval. And each post also." It is moderated, but lightly.

Each post must be written in a uniform style—including the title. If someone tries to post something that doesn't conform with that, "We'll actually reject their post and message them with a note explaining what the norms and expectations are," he says. If they try to post again in violation, Matzner or Myers will consider kicking them out of the group altogether. Recruiters are kicked out. So are "inappropriate" job listings, like an unpaid foreign opportunity. "We just look to the person to make sure it's a legit account," he says. "If we see anyone misbehaving, we remove them from the group." About one person a month is removed, on average.

We know, we know—it's difficult to tell someone no or to kick them off a list. And as community builders, we naturally want to make our people happy. But don't be afraid to be a stickler for the rules in groups you create. Think about the greater good! Most groups fail to become truly valuable to the people in them because nobody is steering the ship. It's up to you to put on the captain's hat and keep things in shipshape order.

Picking a Platform

People shine in different areas. Some people are really great one-on-one. Others are better digitally. Still others know how to work the room and are great at a dinner party. The point is—figure out which area best showcases your strengths, and then work within that. That should be your main platform— where you shine. Which doesn't mean you don't want to use other platforms. It just means that as a leader, you should always begin in the area you are most comfortable.

Schedule engagements to maintain communication so the group takes on a life of its own. Let's say you're doing a Facebook forum. You know that on every Thursday, you want to make sure that you're checking in with the community. If you are looking for staff, post your staff needs on Thursdays. Thursday is your day. Why do this? Because you are building a system wherein you know you'll do the same ask or post in a forum, so it builds legacy and history. The community can then take on a life of its own beyond you.

CHAPTER 15

GOOGLE-PROOFING YOUR REPUTATION

Whenever you're introduced to new people or reach out to meet new people, the first thing they'll do is type your name into Google. Which means that potential relationships can be made or broken based on the first page of a Google search.

Think about that. You can be someone who has robust search findings filled with strong content, press, and relevant social media postings, or it can be bare—or, worse, in select cases, it can have negative results based on past indiscretions or untruths.

The point is, we aren't saying you should use black-hat SEO (shady, frowned-upon strategies) tactics to scrub the Web, but we are saying that if you're going to put a lot of time into building and nurturing relationships, it is probably best to make sure that your best digital footprint is put forward. In short, the five-second Google-search smell check that people will do on you matters . . . a lot.

Second, not only is it important to manage your reputation, but the content people find about you has the opportunity to produce a warmer, friendlier first impression or interaction. What's written about you in the press or by bloggers, what you share or what you publish, paints a picture about who you are and what you stand for. It amplifies your thesis. The right context about you can help people you seek to meet or know better get a sense of you quickly—leading to greater results in your initial encounters. It can also make people more interested in meeting you faster. In a busy world, having no digital footprint, or a poor one, doesn't necessarily scream "priority" to others. The reverse, however, has the chance to make a whole different kind of first impression—one that can make your actual in-person first impression far better and more fulfilling.

Reputation matters. Everything you say, everything you do, everything you tweet or like or post broadcasts a piece of yourself. Whether you like it or not, other people will judge that piece very harshly. The digital world is unforgiving. If you don't believe us, just ask any of the people mentioned in Jon Ronson's book *So You've Been Publicly Shamed*, which is about people whose lives were pretty much ruined because of one erroneous tweet. Or a badly titled Instagram photo. Or a poorly timed joke.

You could also talk to our good friend Pete Kistler, who has personal experience with this on a few different levels. Kistler is the cofounder of BrandYourself, a reputation-management company. He built his company out of necessity. During his senior year at Syracuse University, he did what most college kids do and began applying for jobs. He was a good student and figured he'd get at least some interest. But that's not what happened—no one bit. He didn't understand why, so he took to the Web to do some sleuthing.

That's when he discovered that there was *another* Pete Kistler dominating search-engine results. But this Pete Kistler wasn't an earnest young student seeking an entry-level position; he was a criminal. When employers Googled "Pete Kistler," they didn't stumble upon an impressive soon-to-be college grad ready to dominate the business world, but found a guy with an entirely different rap sheet. Not that any of the companies knew the difference. As far as they were concerned, there was one Pete Kistler, and they didn't want him anywhere near their company, not even sweeping floors.

The experience was unnerving, to say the least. But it inspired (good) Pete Kistler to do two things: to try to fix his reputation and to launch BrandYourself with his friend Patrick Ambron. "Everything we do is now recorded online forever, which means we need more tools to make sure this doesn't harm us," says Ambron. "We now have the technology to track and store all that activity. That means everything we post on Facebook or Twitter and every item we search for, website we visit, online transaction we make, and conversation we have through text or messenger exists *somewhere*. A Facebook-status update you made years ago may eventually get you fired. Even more scary, a private email or message you sent to a friend—even if you deleted it—could come back and bite you."

What this translates to is pretty basic: If your online reputation is a disaster, you most likely won't get the gig. Or the meeting. Or the opportunity. Sad to say, but we are all, each one of us, one bad Google search result away from losing someone's trust.

Still don't believe us? Check out these stats, courtesy of BrandYourself:

- 82 percent of business decision makers said that presence in search results was an influential factor when vetting people online.
- 42 percent of the online US adults who looked somebody up in a search engine looked someone up before deciding to do business with them.
- 27 percent have searched for someone they met in a professional setting, such as a networking event.
- 23 percent of online US adults who have searched someone online have looked up a coworker.

If you're not mindful of the way the world perceives you online, then you're leaving a lot to chance. And what have we learned about Superconnectors? That they do not leave anything to chance, or happenstance, or any other -*ance* word. If you don't control what people see about you online, someone else will. Which means that you must be in charge of your own story. Because what it boils down to is what people see when they Google your name. And you want it to be positive.

Good Versus Bad Context

If you've been in business during this epoch, chances are you've been on the receiving end of a bad Google result. We have, and we'd be lying if we didn't admit that it hurt our business and personal relationships (not to mention our self-esteem). No one wants to discover that their reputation has taken a huge wallop.

But there are right ways and wrong ways of handling less than awesome information about yourself. A few years ago, for example, a Reddit thread popped up in which a prospective YEC member asked if any other Redditors saw value in our organization. Several people chimed in with scathing reviews, using phrases that included the lovely statement "Money down the drain." *Ouch.* It was frustrating and painful, especially because on Reddit anonymity is a norm. We didn't even have a way to validate if the people leaving the biting remarks were actual past or current members. We were pretty confident they were Internet trolls, but still. You never know.

So what's a person to do? We could have easily gotten defensive, but that would have just given credence to the commenters. We could have ignored them altogether, but that would have made it seem like we didn't care. Which we did. *A lot.* We knew that these types of posts tend to rank high in search results. If untreated, there's always the potential for unwanted vitality.

Instead, we found a middle ground, and Ryan responded to each negative commenter with something like this:

> Sorry to hear about your experience so far as a member. I can't find a GEORGE CLOONEY in our YEC database. I assume this is an alias. Would love to connect over email and see what we can do to make your experience everything

that it should be. Email me anytime at [. . .], and we will figure it out.

Ryan's goal was to acknowledge the person's negative experience, while also pointing out in a friendly way that he couldn't validate that he was an *actual* member. It also showed others who saw the thread that we cared so deeply about customer support that an actual company head was reaching out. No one was expecting a decent human response from one of the "higher-ups." Nor did they think anyone was really going to try to listen. But Ryan did.

You'll also notice that nowhere in Ryan's response did he act defensively. "That would have just exacerbated the situation and opened the door for more scrutiny," says Ryan. "People don't like to be called out on being wrong, especially when they are, and especially online anonymously, where there are very few consequences."

Ryan ended his comment with a general message for anyone who happened to Google YEC and found this Reddit thread:

> I'm one of the cofounders of YEC. Happy to speak to anyone who is interested in membership and has questions. You can email me directly at [___]. I'll be honest about whether I think YEC would be valuable to you and your business.

To this day, the few minutes he spent writing a response put him in contact with prospective YEC members at least a couple of times per month and have led to tens of thousands of dollars in new business.

Instead of getting worked up over bad reviews or bad context, you should use them as an opportunity to show what you really stand for, take the conversation elsewhere, and own the opportunity to paint a more accurate picture.

Bad Context

Ryan's response was a strong example of adding "good context" in response to bad context. Bad context after bad context would be when, say, you get into a Twitter war with a random person you have never met. Twitter, as we all know, is highly traceable; it lives forever. Even if you erase it, there can still be trails. Once something's out there, it's out there forever. You don't want this, especially if your responses aren't examples of your most shining moments.

Scott is the go-to guy on this subject. He has been told that when he gets mad, he can be a little, er, scary. In 2012 we started the #FixYoungAmerica movement, something that we were especially proud of. #FixYoungAmerica was an initiative and book whose goal was, in short, to inspire young people and leaders to work together to spark an "entrepreneurial revolution," as we called it.

After a story about it was published in the *New York Times*, *Salon* wrote a follow-up—a screed, frankly—against Scott and YEC. It was a brutal, one-sided piece. But instead of taking Ryan's approach, Scott went full-on bull in a China shop in the comments section. He attacked the journalist and the article as well as the commenters who were commenting on his comments. "I was so heated, Ryan literally had to call me to tell me to stop writing," says Scott. "Looking back, I was incredibly foolish. I looked immature and petty. And my actions caused many reactions that only made the situation worse. I both created and caused bad context, all because I handled the situation incredibly poorly." Bad context begets more bad context when you let it.

But he learned a lesson: "Never do anything to give the wrong impression about who you are," he says. "Sometimes the best reputation management is about what people say you *aren't* versus what they say you are."

You are constantly building a narrative that people believe in, buy into, and convey to others on your behalf. Your reputation shouldn't be forced or crafted via marketing messages. Rather, it should be natural, simple, and compelling. Said another way: it displays the best you because it is the *real* you.

"Reputation is something much more core—it's who you are in the eyes of others," says Adam Grant. "And what matters there, ultimately, is not visibility or prominence or positivity, but sincerity."

What Does Successful Reputation Management Look Like?

The more context-rich information you put out about yourself and your thesis, the better information you're supplying other people. This will help them get to know who you are and what you stand for before you meet them—which is likely to make for a better encounter.

Likewise, it might also help others opt themselves *out* of meeting with you, as they don't necessarily see alignment. Since time is such a commodity, it's best to know these things up-front so as not to waste precious minutes doing things you don't want to do.

"There are things that can pop up that really hurt your career," says Patrick Ambron of BrandYourself. "On the other end, the better you look online, the more of an edge you get, whether you like it or not. It's not always the best person who gets the job. It's the best person who's also good at promoting themselves, because we look so much online. And on both of those ends, if you think about it, and we can do so case by case, on the risky end it's important to know that no matter how responsible you are, something bad can happen to you online."

According to Ambron, research shows that if you have four or five highly visible things out, your opportunities increase like crazy. On the other end, one bad thing can really put your career off the rails.

So what should you be doing to manage your reputation? Other than the obvious (that would be not posting stupid stuff), you want to be proactive, "even if you think you've got nothing to hide or you're very responsible," says Ambron. "Because a bad thing can happen to anybody and hurt their career." Also, he points out, anyone can say anything about you on the Web, and it doesn't matter whether it's true.

Since you want to be vigilant about what's out there about you, you've got to do a little self-Googling every so often. Just as bad things happen to good people, bad Internet happens to good people. Rather than running the risk of waking up one day, logging on, discovering that the world thinks O. J. Simpson has a better reputation than you do, and then freaking out, you should take action before it reaches that point.

To start, you want to do an audit of what's already out there about you. "A lot of people have risk factors that they don't even realize, so Google yourself and then go through your

social media accounts and try to delete things that raise flags,"
says Ambron. What are those flag raisers? Oh, you know—
shots of you doing shots or trekking naked through the streets
of Manhattan. Or using bigoted or sexist language. "A lot of
people don't realize, you know, if they're making jokes to their
friend's wall or something, it's available to everybody," he says.

After taking stock of what's out there, you can determine a
course of action. If it's something negative, delete it. If deleting
it is not an option, you want to make sure there's positive content out there to replace the unwanted information. "Dedicat-
ing an hour or two a month to the handful of properties you've
decided to be on can, as long as you're organized, really have a
giant impact," says Ambron. "As long as you don't have some
abnormally complicated situation, just spending two hours every single month can go a long way."

When Kistler and Ambron were trying to overhaul Kistler's Web presence, they chose ten to fifteen platforms that
they thought would be good for him, including a personal
website (petekistler.com), Twitter, Quora, LinkedIn, and Slide-
Share. Medium.com is another great platform that ranks well
in Google if you publish a few strong posts. As a musician, he
also built out his Soundcloud and YouTube, which rank very
well if you publish a few songs or videos.

Kistler offered to guest blog pro bono about one of his
passions, personal branding, for two websites that already had
excellent Google rankings, the Official Blog of the Syracuse
University iSchool and the Personal Branding Blog. "By writing thoughtful content and publishing it on well-established
platforms, I benefited from the authority their domain names

had already established in search engines. By linking from them to a few of my top newly created profiles, I funneled some extra relevance into those new profiles. My guest-blogger profiles on those sites also ranked well by themselves, which was great, because people could quickly find my articles and see that I was actively writing useful content about my field."

Then they filled those out with positive information about him, making sure to list projects he worked on, along with information, photos, and videos. "You want to make sure that stuff is rich with content, so Google knows it's really a kind of rich source of information about the topic at hand, in this case Pete's name," Ambron says.

After that, spend a few hours each month keeping them up-to-date by blogging, tweeting, and making presentations. In Kistler's case, "That was enough to really start to own those results."

But beware: Many people decide that they have to be superactive on Twitter, Facebook, or Instagram, and so they blog on a daily basis. They start producing rather shoddy posts, and guess what? Their reputation takes a major hit. Or worse—they start out strong and then burn themselves out overdoing it and eventually stop altogether. "You see people kind of think they have to be everywhere," says Ambron. "And sometimes it gets in their way."

How to Build Your Personal Website

Forgive us if we sound like your mother, but we want you to spend your money wisely. Ryan recently mentored a young entrepreneur who spent two thousand dollars to build a website, just to "build his brand." It wasn't his fault: he truly knew nothing about tech. He didn't know that launching a website was so incredibly simple these days that your grandmother could do it. Instead, he got taken advantage of by a development agency that sold him on stuff he didn't need, at least in these early stages of his business. (This—ahem—is a good example of how having a great, diverse community of people in your corner would have been valuable. Had he met Ryan earlier, Ryan would have steered him clear of this idea.) With all due respect, that was not smart, which Ryan (gently) counseled him.

Ryan recently rebuilt his website in preparation for this book for a total of . . . forty-six dollars. He found a WordPress (one of the most popular platforms out there for website producers) theme on ThemeForest.com, whipped out his credit card, and within minutes had a new design that was 99 percent ready to go. Only thing left to do was install it, which the producer of the theme gladly helped him do at no additional charge! Spending two thousand dollars is throwing money down the drain.

But the young entrepreneur cared more about the look and feel of his site than what he was saying and the content and context he was sharing. He wasted a ton of time and money building a picture-perfect website rather than getting out there, building his community, nurturing relationships, and growing his business. This is a mistake many people make when they start building a website, whether for business or for personal branding purposes. And this critical error often leads to a "failure to launch" moment.

Here's what's most critical when you build your personal website:

The content: What does it say about you? Is it honest about who you are, and does it quickly tell the website visitor what you want them to know?

Aesthetics: Does it look nice? Do you have a photo of yourself that's somewhat professional or at least is aligned with who you are? For example, you won't see a suit-and-tie corporate-y photo of Ryan on ryanpaugh.com. He's sitting at a restaurant, wearing a beanie, and drinking a delicious stout with a foam mustache across his lip. But that's who he is, and in his world he can get away with that. You? Maybe. Maybe not.

Connection point: Is it clear how and why people should connect with you? If your website doesn't do something to connect you with people and the opportunities that come along with them, then you're missing something. This is commonly referred to as a "call to action," and it should be one of the most prominent graphics on your website. Eyeballs should be drawn to it like thumbs to an iPhone.

Social proof: We'll get into this much deeper in a moment, but social proof is the evidence that shows people are who they say they are and that they're the sort of person you want to do business with. On Scott's website, scottdgerber.com, he lists all of his press to make sure people instantly see his credibility and can read about what he does from validated sources (and not just his family—or Ryan).

But you don't need to be a media mogul to show social proof. Ryan, for example, isn't nearly as involved in the media landscape as Scott is. He fills in the gaps with thoughtful testimonials from colleagues he has worked with throughout the years. And in some ways, this is a strategy more aligned with who Ryan is anyway. What *real* people say matters more to the community-building nature of his work. From there, think about the additional content you can create to make your website more appealing to the Google gods. As Ambron noted earlier, search engines scour the Web for sites with regularly updated content. For example:

A blog: If you can manage one and keep a regular schedule of at least once per month, a blog is a great way to give your website the ongoing pulse it needs to rank in search results.

Additional pages: Adding depth to your site helps, too. A standard "About" page is good, but we've seen people take it a step further and develop "Fun Facts" about themselves or build a really powerful resource-driven page chock-full of info about a topic that the person wants to rank high for.

Search-engine optimization, or the crazy dark art of ranking in Google, sounds scary, but there are a lot of basics you can implement that are good enough for 99.9 percent of the population. If you use WordPress, you can even download a plugin like the All in One SEO that does most of the work for you.

CHAPTER 16

ARE YOU A CREATOR OR A CURATOR?

Connectors aim to be known not by everyone in the universe, but rather by the right crowd of individuals who will share their goals and value systems. The "right" community.

Everyone should create some form of real estate to call their own. It doesn't matter if it's based on original or curated content—the bigger issue is the type of medium you use. Which one is right for your audience: Writing? Podcasting? Video? Infographics? Sketch notes?

Gary Vaynerchuk, a best-selling author, angel investor, and the CEO of VaynerMedia, believes that people should always decide what type of content would best fit *their* skill sets. If you are better verbally than on paper, then you might want to think about a podcast. If you are an expert doodler, then maybe you want to draw your message and post your big ideas on more visual platforms like Instagram or Pinterest. However, remember that the content you are providing is for your audience, not yourself. If you are known for your amazing webcasts, continue them. Vaynerchuk also believes that business owners should tailor their content to the platform it's published on.

But you also need to know which type of person you are. Do you gather and share the best content for your network, or do you see yourself as a creator of such high-value content?

Both curators and creators are important. A curator makes the world less noisy and provides a valuable service by shepherding the cream to the top. But you need to be excellent at it to keep people engaged.

Creators have the ability to bring new ideas or thinking and create a lot of value. But similarly, if you aren't great at it, you just end up making more noise. We recommend people pick a medium to create content as it leaves a record (an "artifact," in earlier book parlance, if you will).

Some of the newsletters that Adam Grant subscribes to are written by people who don't say a single thing themselves but have a really good case around topics that he is curious to learn more about. "I value their judgment about what I should be reading, what I should be watching, whom I should be listening to," he says. "It's meta sharing: helping to guide people about what else to pay attention to and what to consume that's worthwhile."

One thought-provoking article that provides real, tactical, actionable advice to someone in need can give years of steady support for you and your business. It makes you a thought leader and someone worth doing business with. "People wander around believing that if they only meet more brilliant amazing important people, their work will improve," says Grant. "And the reality is that it's hard to engage with those people and learn from them unless you put something interesting and meaningful out into the world to begin with. That's what attracts their attention. When people say, 'It's not what you know, it's who you know,' I would say, 'Actually, who you know is often a function of what you know and, even further, what you share.'"

How to Build Social Proof

It's no secret that word of mouth—and word of Web—is a businessperson's best friend. Just look at all the options we have to review products. Want to book a hotel? Just see what people are saying on TripAdvisor. Looking for a good doctor? Check out Healthgrades. And so on. They are testimonials, and they help people make informed decisions.

We go to these websites because we want to hear what other customers have to say. We want their recommendations on where to go and, more important, where not to go. (Businesses are well aware of this; it's why they sometimes offer incentives for you to post something nice about them.)

But people need social proof, too. Without it life becomes much more difficult, especially if you are trying to advance your career.

At its core, social proof is the stuff on the Web that validates you. Not just how you use logos on your site or email signature—that's a benefit of social proof, but not the social proof itself. The social proof is that there are independent verifiable things in the world about you that you didn't game or pay for. Your ability to showcase and package them is very important, but only after you've earned the accreditations in the first place.

When Jared Kleinert sent a cold email to Keith Ferrazzi, he already had some pretty good credentials. There was his soon-to-be-published book, *2 Billion Under 20*, from St. Martin's. There was the TEDx talk he had given from his research. And he had great results from his work with a couple of VC-backed startups. His initial email to Ferrazzi "showed the social proof of being a TEDx speaker and being an author to be," he says. "That, I think, cuts out from the rest of the pack. It separates me from the noise that is his inbox."

Working with Ferrazzi gave him only more credibility. "He gave me his testimonial and support initially," he says. "I was able to craft a case study off the work I had done for him."

Social proof comes in a variety of forms: either you write for a noteworthy outlet, they write about you, you receive an accolade or award, or someone of note writes about you.

Whatever you do, do not try to fake social proof—it will backfire and cause problems for you. Nor should you use "bad" or "underwhelming" social proof. Some people are so hungry to get a logo or something on their site to validate them, they will literally use sites they've been featured on that are simply not known or unimpressive. This has the reverse effect. Better to take the proper time to get the right success under you and then seek out the things that will truly represent you best. Social proof works both ways, and you don't want the negative version.

"People should build real competence and build a great reputation behind their personal brand before they go for having a personal brand that is also well known," says Kleinert. "You should establish a great body of work that is impressive in your industry before you necessarily go for having a ton of people know about you. If it happens in unison, awesome."

Pitching Yourself as a Contributor

We have worked with countless professionals who saw the content marketing space as a provocative way to grow their business, but their expectations of how it works were all wrong. Most people think that by getting published in a name-recognizable media outlet, traffic will automatically flock to your website and people will take interest in whatever value you have to provide. Nope.

In fact, most pieces of content create little to no traffic to your site, leaving anyone who came in with this expectation convinced that creating content is a complete waste of time. This isn't true, but we understand the frustration.

When you pitch media, you have no say over the end product. You don't control the journalist's angle, nor do you know how they'll personally feel about your expertise or what you have to say. However, being a contributor enables you to voice your thoughts in your words (so long as the editor you work with finds it noteworthy and not advertorial, that is).

Scott built his entire early career pitching media outlets or blogs and writing highly valuable content on topics of interest to him (his thesis: youth entrepreneurship). This content then led journalists and television networks to reach out to him based on what he'd written and his stated expertise. By putting his own thoughts and words out there, he was able to specifically convey his points. Simultaneously, as his content became refined, his access to even better blogs and media outlets increased dramatically. His consistency and point of view helped open many doors. This then led to strong social proof (e.g., "As seen on XYZ" or "Read my column on XYZ!") and thousands of articles being written about YEC over the years.

People often try to pitch the press too early, and it falls on deaf ears. Journalists want to interview subjects with strong credentials and newsworthy stories. By starting on your own platform and then expanding into being a contributor, you begin to build a public track record and narrative. You become accredited by others, which leads to more prestigious organizations taking note. And so on and so on.

Pitching to be a contributor isn't easy, but today, with the ever-shifting media landscape, it certainly isn't impossible. As media outlets look for new ways to monetize their business model, they are trying to find ways to increase their page views and ad revenue with less staff. This has led to a natural increase in contributors being utilized to deliver highly relevant, valuable content.

Once you have some pieces written (or a podcast or video or whatever your preference of media platform), it's best to research the right editors at publications that have contributor programs and reach out. Don't necessarily start with the absolute top outlets in the world, but work your way up. Make sure to demonstrate why your voice and perspective are different and why they will resonate based on what's happening in the world. Scott started pitching to be a contributor before it was a thing. He didn't have any journalism background or special access. Yet within two years of consistency and relationship development, he ended up contributing to dozens of media outlets, ranging from CNN to the *Wall Street Journal* to *Forbes*. Not only will you end up with valuable bylines where you have more control over the final content, but media platforms are some of the highest-ranking sites for SEO on the Web. Most media sites will be at the top of Google—offering you strong visibility, social proof, and great content to share.

One of our most coveted pieces is a blog post Scott wrote for the *Huffington Post* about why professional organizations are the next big frontier for publishers. That piece was read by many prospective partners of ours during the courting process. While the content didn't receive tens of thousands of views, the few hundred it did get came from a very high concentration of the exact people we wanted to meet and know. Plus, when potential partners were vetting us, they could find this article credited to Scott's name. Before he even walked in the door, he had helped to define his belief system, what he cares about, what he does, and more. This made the initial interaction warmer and friendlier.

Pitching Contributors Rather Than Staff Writers

If you recall, Jared Kleinert was featured in a September 6, 2015, article in *USA Today*, which called him—someone who started out knowing only a former white-collar convict in the business world—"the Most Connected Millennial." How did he end up in that publication? By being friends with the writer. "I didn't actually know that he was a writer before that publication, as we were building a friendship," he stresses. "There are a few things to point out from that experience. One is, don't just meet people because there's a transaction that they could offer you. Build real friendships with the right people."

Kleinert knew that what mattered more was not who wrote the article but where it was published. When he was just starting out, "I would look to pitch to people who are contributors—that is, freelancers who are not on staff—to different outlets like *USA Today* or *Forbes* or *Inc.* or *Entrepreneur*," he says. "Those people, unlike staff writers and journalists, have other jobs. If you can work with them to craft pieces that are either about you or mention you as an expert, you're doing those contributors a service by helping them make great content that would grow their brands when they get traffic and saving them time in the process."

Using Knowledge Gaps to Build Reputation

Abby Binder has also been very smart about her career and how she spends her money. Binder runs Abby Windows, an exterior remodeling firm in Milwaukee and Boston. She's been at it for twelve years and is known as one of the good ones. Once they get over their shock that she is—yes!—a woman in a male-dominated field, customers love her. She is honest, direct, and fair, and her reputation reflects this.

She also began hosting a monthly radio call-in show, where people considering remodeling their homes or apartments can ask questions. Those people in many cases transform into clients, as do listeners who view her as an authority in the home-improvement space because she's on the radio. The secret is, though, *anyone can do this*. That means you!

People assume that these types of opportunities are only for the privileged. Well, people would be wrong. Binder and others like her are simply the ones who have the gusto to go out there and talk to people, make a bold ask, and see what happens. If you want a radio show, you can go out and get one. Guaranteed. The question you have to ask yourself is, is that the right avenue to meet the people that I care about? If the answer is yes, great! Get out there, be brazen, and make it happen for yourself.

Binder also makes appearances on *Mr. Fix It*, another caller-based show on a local station in Milwaukee. "One caller had a roofing gable bend and someone uncovered it, and now her attic is getting condensation," she recalls. "I knew right away it was a ventilation issue. So, we helped out. My goal was to have her call me, and we fixed it."

While radio is a great platform, the context, knowledge sharing, and expertise she offers are what enable her to build relationships with new clients and partners. They're attracted to her because she is authentic in her caring, sharing, and expertise. So it's not surprising that while half of her business comes from these shows, the other half comes from referrals.

Solidifying Reputation by (Content) Association

Earlier we talked about the power of association. You can get equal value from whom your *content* associates with.

The best connectors don't just extrapolate their own thoughts; they also build content engines that attract amazing people who will, in turn, share their thoughts. The best connectors build their own content engines and real estate by doing what they do best: telling other people's stories. For example: Dan Schawbel with his blog interviews. Lewis Howes with his podcasts. Michael Ellsberg with his book. Scott when he did a video show called *Founders Forum* with *Inc.* magazine.

You are using all of the tools we have taught (e.g., credibility through association, giving value, and so forth) and packing it in the form of content. This also enhances your digital footprint, shows you have access, and enables you to build systems to support this machine so you don't do what most folks do when it comes to content—which is to write three posts and then quit.

The substance that's geared toward the right people, a strong digital footprint, and so on: we don't want to get into the marketing-world lingo or thought process, as those aren't the goals we are talking about. It's about creating new real estate that better defines you to the world and attracts the right people to your community.

In general, most people make the mistake of thinking that content must be about promoting themselves and their professional interests. But really, the best way to take advantage of writing, whether on your own blog or in a world-renowned publication, is to set yourself up as the expert or thought leader for that thing you really want to be known for.

CHAPTER 17

YES, YOU CAN BE A SUPERCONNECTOR *AND* PAY YOUR BILLS (AND THEN SOME)

If this were a traditional business book, now would be the time when we'd tell you how to profit from your Superconnectedness. In other words, how to translate everything we've told you into big bucks. But as you've probably gathered by now, this is not a traditional networking book.

Like everything else in life, "profiting" means different things to different people. To some people, it's about financial reward. To others, it might mean time saved. To still others, it's about career success. "Profiting" could also be a combination of several things. There is no right answer; we all have different

needs and goals, and they all change over time. So your definition of profiting might also evolve over time.

But here's the thing about connecting: it's not transactional. You can't become a connector with the goal of making
a dollar. As Endeavor founder and CEO Linda Rottenberg says,
"Networks work when they are built on trust, give-and-take,
and long-term attitudes. Where they break down is when they
get transactional and people think, 'What can I get out of it for
me?' When it's just transaction and getting ahead and no one
has an ethos of paying it forward, communities break down."

David Cohen, of Techstars, does not believe that individual relationships should come with a financial ROI. But "if you
want to think of it as a portfolio of relationships that have an
ROI, I don't have any objection to that," he says. "I have many
relationships that I put energy and effort into so that in aggregate, there will be an ROI. But it's not about the individual
interaction; it's about the network of interactions viewed as a
whole."

As Wharton professor Adam Grant says, everyone needs to
set up a "line" of where they give and where they make money.
And you have to make sure that others clearly understand the
difference. "I've seen this in the community of authors, for
example, of people saying, 'Look, I don't do free speaking engagements, but I do write for free,'" he says. "Or 'I don't do free
consulting, but I'll give feedback on a written document sometimes when somebody asks.' Just clearly demarcating what you
charge for and what you don't is kind of an interesting strategy."

Part of your purpose is setting clear boundaries of what
you're in a position to give, what you're not in a position to

give, and what you won't or can't give because it would hurt you to do so. Before you can figure out how you want to profit, you have to discern *why* you want to be a connector and then align your goals with that.

You also want to use your time wisely. Think about it. We're all juggling twelve different things at once; you have to pick and choose where to focus your energy. "I don't think that the idea of investing your time has to be a negative or transactional way of thinking about it," says Michael Ellsberg, "as long as you're taking the broader view of investing your time with a return of value for yourself, for the other person, and for your values and your mission in the world."

Trust in Other People's Judgment

While you'll get many "opportunities" from your network, depending on whom you talk to, you need to almost score the relationship. How long and how well do you know the other person? What's your track record with them? Do you trust that they have your best interests at heart?

Ingrid Vanderveldt (IV) built and sold two ventures and helped countless other entrepreneurs build, grow, and exit theirs. She also became the first-ever entrepreneur-in-residence (EIR) at Dell. In that role, she used what she learned "in the trenches" of business to help other entrepreneurs, and now she is on a mission to empower a billion women by 2020.

Her path to EIR started with an almost declined invitation. Due to a hectic schedule, Vanderveldt would field dozens of invitations a week. She had to pick and choose which ones were worth her time. So when she was invited to the Dell Women's

Entrepreneur Network (DWEN), she was ready to skip it due to other obligations—until a longtime friend and fellow entrepreneur, Heidi Messer, called her and said, "You really *need* to do this, IV." IV always trusted Heidi's judgment, and so she went. She ended up meeting the top brass at Dell, including Steve Felice, Dell's COO, and the relationships she built at DWEN are what led to her EIR gig a year later.

All the Superconnectors we've talked to became connectors to build a community. But with the help of their community, each one of them also made connections that would help them later. When Jon Levy's book came out, he called on the media relationships he had cultivated at his dinners to help him with press. Steve Sims's and John Ruhlin's kindness has netted them millions of dollars in client contracts. Jayson Gaignard's community loves what he built so much, they spend thousands of dollars annually to be a part of his event series. David Cohen's network has enabled him to create one of the top startup accelerators in the world, offering him and his colleagues investment opportunities in some of the premier companies in the world. Jim Pierce built a practice and a community around him. Michael Ellsberg was able to publish a book that went gangbusters for his career. You get the idea.

There is a reason the top businesspeople in the world continue to work together time and again: Trust. Integrity. Powerful bonds. Longer term, successful people are going to want to work with and help other successful people, so it's important that early on, they identify you as someone who has the ambition—and drive—to be ambitious. It's good to have vision, passion, and motivation for what you do. And many people will want to help you achieve that success. You just need to go about it the right way and not bastardize your relationships.

Indeed, we all know people who see others as mere stepping-stones. For them, people are instruments to help them climb the ladder. As soon as they get to where they need to be—boom! They disappear. These are the same sorts of people who call only when they need something. Nothing sucks more than feeling used.

One thing is clear: if you follow the ideas we've laid out in this book, in a few short years you will have assembled the right community of amazing people around you. If you do everything we suggest, many of the right people are going to want your attention or will send things your way. So it's important to consider all the ways in which your Superconnecting skills work for you.

Adam Grant believes that in every workplace, there are three basic kinds of people: givers, takers, and matchers. The most successful *and* least successful people are both givers. How is this possible? The main difference is that the ones on the top have learned to say no sometimes. The ones at the bottom try to do for everybody. They give and give and get nothing in return. That is decidedly not smart. "It's about being thoughtful about who you help, how you help, and when you help," says Grant.

> What we see with failed givers is that they try to help all the people all the time with all the requests, and they end up sacrificing their own success as, you know, they devote so much time and energy to help others that they fall behind on their own work. They get exploited by more selfish takers,

and they end up contributing in ways that are actually not all that effective. Whereas what you see with successful givers is they say, "Look, I'm not going to help everybody equally." If somebody has a history or a reputation of selfish behavior, then I'm going to shift more into matching mode and hold them accountable for paying it back or paying it forward. And that way I get to reserve my generosity for people who are fair or are themselves generous.

Bottom line: if you try to be everything to everyone, you likely won't be anything to anyone.

Ryan and I are exceptions to one particular rule: that it's a good idea to build a business out of your community. They rarely succeed. We aren't saying don't do it, but we *are* saying that there are many other, easier, ways to "profit" as a result of your network.

We did not become Superconnectors to make money. We became Superconnectors because we really like introducing people to each other. We live for it. It's second nature to us. But while introductions are a fun endorphin-induced high, the *real* reason we became Superconnectors is because we know that the right people coming together can create wonderful outcomes.

Not only is it beneficial from a business perspective, but it might also be life enhancing. A July 2008 study in the *American Journal of Public Health* found that strong social ties may actually promote brain health. We will probably never know if our lives are extended because Dan Schawbel introduced us, but we *do* know that our lives would have been less full. (So would yours: you wouldn't be reading this book!)

Which doesn't mean that we don't think about money. We're not stupid. We have six children between us, along with mortgages and car payments and dental bills. We want to earn a living, and then some. We would be lying if we said there isn't financial gain to all of this. There certainly can be. However, you don't want to make money off your connections but rather profit as a result of *doing well* by them.

So it's okay to think about money. It's okay to think about yourself to some extent. Profiting should come as a result of aggregate efforts rather than one relationship. It's not that we should be selfish, but we should remain mindful of our own needs as well as other people's. We were eventually able to turn relationship building into a business, but that did not happen for many years and not until we realized that we were good at it.

If you reread this book, you will have noticed that not one person we spoke to said they got into it in order to make a lot of money. They said, "This is my life's passion and purpose. I love it, and if I can help people and also make money, all the better."

Different Ways to Benefit

So how do you make money as a Superconnector? Let's say you are at a job. If you are seen as a team player—that is, someone who will help the organization more effectively—you will have a better chance of climbing the ladder. You'll be seen as integral to the growth of the organization.

"Profiting" comes in a variety of shapes and forms. "Profiting" is not necessarily about financial reward—or any material reward, for that matter. Nor is it about "profiting" from a single transaction.

Anjula Acharia, a partner at Trinity Ventures, an investment firm in San Francisco, benefited greatly by getting a major career opportunity through her network. Acharia came to the United States from England with no contacts at all. But she built a network that created opportunities for her to work with people like Lady Gaga and Britney Spears and struck her first deal in the music business with Edgar Bronfman, then CEO of Warner Music Group.

One of her mentors is visionary music man Jimmy Iovine, the founder of Interscope Records. She met him through venture capitalist Drew Lipsher, and, as she puts it, "He has opened the door to many people for me."

Not long after they met, he gave her a large chunk of change to invest in a startup she was launching called Desi Hits, a media company that produced and distributed entertainment for the South Asian community. A few months later, she and Iovine were sitting at the St. Regis hotel in New York. That's when he told her the truth: that the startup wasn't going to work out and that he was going to stop funding it. But, he stressed, he *was* investing in her.

Iovine was right. Desi Hits didn't work out the way Acharia wanted it to, at least not financially. But it *did* help her hone herself as an entrepreneur, and through it she expanded her network. Since then, she and Iovine have invested in other projects, most notably launching the career of Bollywood actress Priyanka Chopra in the United States. Chopra, who starred in *Quantico*, became the first South Asian network TV drama star. She made history. And so did Acharia.

CHAPTER 18

HOW TO MAKE A SMART ASK AS A SUPERCONNECTOR

We know this sounds like a no-brainer: *Who doesn't know how to ask for something? You open your mouth and spew. Right?*

Wrong.

Most people are terrible askers. They don't realize that there is a methodology to making an ask. While some people believe in chance or luck, Superconnectors use *intention*. After all, if you go around asking everyone you know for help, or if you make the wrong ask at the wrong time, it can seem transactional. Or you could risk making a gross error in judgment. You can say the wrong thing. Or come off with bad or underhanded intentions. So you want to make sure the people you're making asks of share your values, goals, and vision.

Some of the world's biggest deals and careers have been built on nothing more than smart asks and inbound referrals.

These are the two biggest tools a connector has in their arsenal. These are the simple yet effective ways connectors receive value. They are the meat and potatoes. But though these tools seem simple, most people don't have a clue how to use them right. That's because they tend to view relationships transactionally, which gets them nowhere.

Remember David Hassell? He's the guy who ran the Mansion Series out of his (ginormous) San Francisco home. He had recently started a company called 15Five, an intercompany employee-feedback system. He raised capital from forty different investors in sixty days. Yes: two months. How did he do it?

By never treating people as if they were just oversize wallets. "Your relationships and your connections aren't necessarily the place to make money," says Hassell. "In some cases they can be, but I don't think about relationships transactionally. Instead, I view them as one source of power or capital that can help in the process of creating other things."

Many of the people who invested in his company were strangers to him, who signed on after one twenty-minute phone call. But his reputation—and connections—proved his viability. He was a known quantity, trusted. "And trust is transferable," he says. "Say I know an investor who's close with someone I'm close with, and they have a tight relationship and I have a tight relationship with the person. Now, the investor has never heard of me, doesn't know my name, we've never met, but when this person introduces me and says, 'Look, I've known Dave for three years. He and I have done X, Y, and Z. He's a great guy, very trustworthy,' it's like the trust he's built with this investor now transfers to me." And all he had to do was ask.

Here are some things that have happened to us as a result of our asks:

- We were introduced to a very specific chief executive and in turn ended up with a deal that has since generated millions of dollars with millions more to come.
- We have been introduced to countless vendors that have served us incredibly well over the years—and helped us avoid huge time sucks and bad vendor experiences.
- YEC was the lead feature story on the cover of the *New York Times* Sunday Business section (twice).
- We raised several million dollars in funding for our business.
- We were able to get an A-list celebrity to attend one of our YEC events at no cost to us (and he had a fantastic time).
- The right ask to someone in Scott's network (a "tweet" ask, no less) resulted in a new partnership that will generate millions of dollars.

All this because we asked the right someone at the right time for the right help.

Of course, you've got to be—dare we say it—self-aware. And yes, that requires a bit of inventory. Here are some questions to ask yourself:

Is the person I'm going to make an ask of the right person to make the intro I'm seeking? Just because someone can help or wants to help doesn't mean they should or that they'll be received by the end party positively.

Does someone who does not understand anything about my industry or business, or whatever, understand my ask? Basically, do people think I'm being clear? What context am I not offering that I should? After all, if I want to talk to someone in my city but I don't make that clear, I can end up getting an intro to someone in a different city—which ultimately makes for a bad experience for everyone, from the person I'm being introduced to to the person who made the intro on my behalf.

Can I figure this challenge out myself or through an available means so I don't waste social capital on a simple ask? The point is, ASSESS, ASSESS, ASSESS! Don't just turn and speak; don't make random requests. Analyze, critique, and validate—then make your ask.

Bad Asks

We once got a call from an entrepreneur in the professional services industry. He was looking for capital.

"What kind?" we asked.

"Angel investor," he replied.

We stopped in our tracks. He had a great business, but angels clearly weren't going to invest, because the investment-return profile wasn't there. It was obvious that he was asking for the wrong kind of capital.

So instead, we offered to introduce him to alternative lend-ers who were not looking to invest in exchange for equity but rather looking to underwrite a loan at a higher interest rate.

He took the loan instead of searching out equity financing, which saved him a ton of time and needless rejection. In the process, he was able to make his business cash flow positive and never raise capital. Had he gone after his original ask, he would likely have spent many months without getting anywhere and gotten only very frustrated, perhaps even developed insecurities about the strength of his business—all because he was making the wrong ask.

The Thoughtless, Lazy Ask

Ryan's pet peeve is when someone says, "Does anyone know someone at X Company?" and then gives zero info beyond that. Ryan will think, "Um, yeah, maybe I do. But why should I con-nect you? What value do you bring? And are you going to use the connection I make for you in a genuine, mutually benefi-cial purpose or simply try to sell them on something they don't need?" It's a totally vague, useless question.

If you're the one looking for help, you must be specific about your needs. Some people don't want to go into detail be-cause they believe that whatever they're working on is top se-cret. We understand why you wouldn't want to broadcast your project to the world. But if you're asking a favor of someone and not willing to be open about what you are looking for, that's a problem. And kinda stupid.

Your ask defines you not only to the person to whom you are asking, but also to the future party who may or may not be connected to you. If you ask for something that sounds nonsensical, you're basically pigeonholing yourself and for sure setting a bad impression.

Sometimes people just have poorly thought-out or half-baked asks. Other times people offer a lot of information about themselves but no information about why a connection is synergistic and makes any sense. And sometimes there is a lot of information given but none that's actually relevant.

If you want someone to make an important connection on your behalf, then you give them more information up-front. This goes back to what we talked about earlier as far as doing things—say, conducting certain marketing exercises like spammy emails—that they themselves would never take interest in. The same thing applies here. If you wouldn't help someone who has your ask, or didn't understand what someone with your ask was asking, why would you even pop the question?

For instance, at X Company you may think that the CEO is the one who can solve your problem best, when in reality it's someone three rungs down the ladder. Unless you provided that extra context to someone with an "in" at the company, you'd be connecting to the wrong person—and you'd probably walk away with nada.

Paraag Marathe, chief strategy officer and executive vice president of football operations for the San Francisco 49ers, has pretty strong feelings about this. "I would have to have a number of conversations with somebody before I make an introduction for them," he says. "I get asked all the time, 'Can you make an introduction to this or that person?' A lot of times

I'll say yes, but I'll give it with a caveat that I'm not going to be able to give some really effusive, praiseworthy recommendation because I don't really know you."

How to Make a Good Ask

Make sure your ask is structured and context rich: Remember our discussion about "context" conversations? The conversations that give extra detail around a particular topic? Well, now you are using these protocols on yourself, to make sure you're delivering a robust, context-rich ask that minimizes confusion and maximizes the chances for success.

So, say you're looking to meet a person at a particular company. If you've done your due diligence and you know for a fact that the decision maker you're trying to reach is Paul, then you ask for him and explain why. But rather than saying, "Can you introduce me to Paul Smith at XYZ Company?" you say, "I'm looking to learn what decision makers at enterprise companies in the X industry are looking for when assessing new vendors, so I can better prepare our business's marketing and pitch materials. I know you work with a number of these companies daily. Do you know someone who is a midlevel or senior manager with decision-making ability who might be able to spare fifteen minutes?"

Be concise: If you can't make it clear in thirty seconds what you are looking for and why in a simple, straightforward, and concise manner, don't say anything at all. You should lead with what you are trying to achieve—what the result you are looking for is and not the means by which you want to get there.

Erica Keswin is a workplace strategist, professional dot connector, and founder of the Spaghetti Project, which she calls a "roving homespun huddle." It's a real-live spaghetti meal where people gather together to meet, share some pasta, and talk about what they need. "I tell people, the more specific you can be, the easier it is for people to help you," says Keswin, a former executive recruiter. "You need to do some thinking and have a shtick. The more general the ask, the less likely it is that they're going to say yes and even be able to help you."

Target the right person: You need to find a specific person, type of person, or resource you want to be connected to. One of Scott's most hated questions is "Do you know the CEO of X Company?" That's because it assumes that the top dog is always the right dog, when most times it's the wrong person and, as the potential connector, makes us think that the asker seeks only to meet big names. This is usually a big red flag.

Sometimes there are exceptions to the rule of always having to know exactly what you need when you ask for help. Like when you're asking for mentorship on a topic you don't know the first thing about. In these cases, a little humility in your ask is important. An example: "Hey, Scott and Ryan. I know diddly about community building, but I think it would be a great investment for me to know more to support my business." This is a much better approach than being the sort of person who pretends to know more than they actually do.

Make the other person a "thought partner" with you: You might know what you are looking for. But do you know how to get that end result? If not, who are the people you trust to bring in as "thought partners," people who can help you structure your ask when you aren't exactly sure how to get to the end result?

An example: You may want to get a book published, but going to any publisher might not make sense. Instead of asking a friend who has been published for a direct intro to their editor, it might make more sense to have a conversation with that person to learn the best approach, what makes for the right publisher fit, what a book proposal looks like, and so on. The person might be able to help with an intro if it makes sense, or the advice might help you find the right person to open a door using the new information.

"The people who do the best with asking are the people who do their research and really think about what it is that they want, but also figure out a way to make the other person a 'thought partner' with you," says Michael Roderick.

Setting realistic and achievable expectations: Starting off with a high-reach goal is never a good way to start a relationship. Like time commitments, this can be another reason the other party opts out beforehand. You shouldn't seek a grand slam on call one.

Be clear on the time commitment involved: many people miss this step, and then the party you're looking to connect with ends up opting out, because they assume this will involve a massive time commitment on their part. By making the time commitment clear in your initial ask, the party you want to connect with will become more comfortable with saying yes, because they know what they're saying yes to up-front.

The win-win ask: How did Elliott Bisnow and his team get people to invest $40 million on his mountain retreat? "I asked," he says.

That's true. But he didn't stand on the street corner brandishing a sign saying, "Wanna invest in my mountain?" Instead, he brought the idea to people who would mutually benefit from what he was going to ask them. Everyone Bisnow reached out to shared a common vision and goal. There was no other place out there like what Elliott was envisioning—a mountaintop in Utah!—and so he recruited his community through smart asks.

How to Be Sure You're Making the Right Ask

Before making an ask, there are a series of questions to ask yourself in advance:

> Am I ready to make an ask for someone?
> Is there a high likelihood of success?
> Are you asking the right person?
> How well do you know the person? How well do they
>   know you?
> Have you ever made an ask of this person before? Were
>   they receptive to the ask?
> If they were, what was the outcome? Stellar or
>   mediocre?

Then there's the ask itself, which is also easy to get wrong if you don't take the time to really think it through. If you don't structure your ask, you look silly and unprofessional, and it leaves a bad taste in people's mouths. Is it reasonable or even doable? Can you do it yourself? Is the information readily available? If someone sees a lazy ask, they might think less of you as a person. You don't want to waste social capital on something that's not quite right.

How to Make the Right Ask of the Right Person

Once you are clear that you've found the right person, you need to make sure you are communicating with them in a way that they understand. Some factors to keep in mind:

Do you speak the same language? Oftentimes, when making an ask of someone, you're crossing into uncharted territory, dealing with industrial, geographical, or political landscapes you don't understand. If you don't understand their world even in the most basic of ways, the likelihood of even scratching the surface of getting what you want is low. So you always want to be clear and make sure other people *think* you are being clear. You'd be surprised how many things seem obvious to you but are anything but to the people you are talking to.

Timing: It's a natural extension of speaking the same language. The timing in which you make your ask is critical in both the micro and the macro senses. If you're making an ask of a parent with multiple kids under the age of five, don't call them on the phone at six thirty on a weeknight. If you're making an ask of a top executive at Target, maybe don't do it on Black Friday.

The medium: Before reaching out, find out the most appropriate form of communication for the person you're reaching out to *and* the favor you're looking for. Email, phone call, a tweet, a handwritten letter? In our world, we have created friendships with many tastemakers with large online followings. If, say, we needed their help promoting something through a quick tweet to their network, a quick text or email might be just fine. If we wanted to launch a large multichannel marketing campaign with them that puts heavy time constraints on both their time and ours, well, we damn well better pick up the phone and get more personal. Maybe even meet in person for a cup of coffee . . . or a steak, depending on what you're after (on *your* tab, of course).

Knowing what you actually need and why you need it: A good asker always knows what they want and why they want or need it. And even more, they show up prepared, with detailed information to back it up if they need it.

Superconcierge Steve Sims wholeheartedly agrees with this tactic. "If I want something, it's gotta benefit you," he says. "I've gone to people and said, 'I want this to happen.' My message is transparent. There's a difference between being easy to understand and impossible to misunderstand. I don't want you to ever misunderstand what I want. In LA, no one is direct. But I don't have a half hour to waste. Tell me: What do you have? What do you want to do?"

Conveying your thoughts or message in your own words: Since this is your request, you want to make it as easy as possible for everyone involved. So you should offer to write a short three- to five-sentence email outlining the ask—something that can be easily forwarded. By offering this, you're removing a friction point from the connector and getting your own words in front of the party you're looking to connect with. It's also a great way to ensure that what you're trying to say doesn't get lost in a game of telephone. This puts your best foot forward because it's your foot and has a very high likelihood of being read by the other party based on the relationship that person has with the connector.

Follow Up, but Don't Overpush

As we said earlier in this book, you want to follow up *smartly*. You don't want to overpush or make people feel like "they work for you." Roderick, the teacher turned Broadway producer, recalls the old friend he thought would be a perfect person to get involved in a show that Roderick was working on. So Roderick sent him an email, laying out everything he needed. He didn't hear anything, so he sent another. And then another.

Finally, he received an email back, saying that this guy had "lost his job, that his wife had cancer, that all of these horrible things had happened to him," says Roderick. "It basically taught me a very valuable lesson, which is that if somebody in your network goes cold, you never, never, never reach out asking for something until you know exactly what's going on with them and how their life is and what's happening, because it can be incredibly damaging."

In other words: If you don't hear from someone, don't pester them, tempting though it may be. None of us likes it when our emails go unanswered. But guess what? Sometimes it's not about us.

Now that you know when and how to make an ask, let's go through some things to ensure it's the right move.

Reverse-Engineering Success

Your job is to take on as much of the heavy lifting as possible and to eliminate any possible friction that might impede success. You want to make it as convenient and simple as possible for both the connector and the party you're seeking a connection with to receive and digest your request—and ultimately meet to further discuss and fulfill the ask.

In order to properly reverse-engineer success, you need to troubleshoot an ask and ask yourself one simple question: "Why will my ask fail?" This will help you improve or clarify your ask, dissuade you from making a half-baked or bad ask, and give you the confidence to proceed.

Here's how Ingrid Vanderveldt reverse-engineered a successful ask to get into the role of EIR. When she first went in to pitch Steve Felice, whom she met back at DWEN, she shared with him the vision she had to "empower a billion women by 2020." She knew that the only way to accomplish that vision was through technology. She was seeking a global tech partner to collaborate with who was equally committed to the success of women around the globe.

"My interest was to secure Dell as a partner," Vanderveldt said, "but I also approached the meeting by saying, 'Steve, here is how I can be of service to you all.' I knew Dell cared about women. I knew they cared about entrepreneurs, and at the time they were really known as an enterprise company. But they wanted to change that perception. And I knew that in working together, I could create programs by and for people like me as an entrepreneur, or as a woman, that would authentically connect."

She told Felice, "'I know that I can tap Dell into a community of women and entrepreneurs around the globe who will help you authentically connect to them and ultimately drive business.'"

Vanderveldt pitched Felice on the EIR program. This was how she would be able to drive value and be of service to Dell. Felice saw the potential, and he also shared her vision of helping not only women around the globe but all entrepreneurs in general.

So Dell chose to bring her on board. Felice, along with the help of leaders at Dell like Jennifer "J. J." Davis, provided guidance and insight into what would work for Dell, and IV created the EIR program, soup to nuts. Vanderveldt's agreement with Dell was, "Okay, you help us do what we want to do on the entrepreneur side (and the women's side), and if we are successful at that, it will automatically help achieve the goal that I have for myself."

Vanderveldt says her time at Dell reiterated so much of what she had learned in working on big ideas in life and in business. "The people who are doing big things in the world, who are authentic connectors, who are people who fundamentally show up and say, 'Here is how I can help *you*, here's how you can help me, and here are the timeline and the deliverable,'" she says. "Those are the people that tie the service and the ROI piece into the same interaction to get the result they want. And it's a win-win for both sides."

Ingrid was able to achieve her goal of having Dell's support, which she credits as key to being able to do the work she does today with Empowering a Billion Women by 2020. With EBW2020, she now has a company that came about as a result of her services there. And she did it all by reverse-engineering her success.

CHAPTER 19

HOW TO BUILD CONSISTENT REFERRALS

As a Superconnector, over time your community will naturally make referrals. Your job is to train people on what makes for great referrals and build natural moments which your network refers to regularly.

Investing in Your Own Referral Network

The more you invest your time, focus on your anchors and others whom you trust, and rely on referrals, the better quality your inbound referrals will be. If you're the local accountant like Jim Pierce, it's probably best to build relationships with people you deem to be the best service providers in your area, from lawyers to doctors to landscapers. People you share an audience or customer base with. By consistently working with the best, and more important heavily investing in the relationships beyond surface-level conversations, you begin to build a referral network. We've found that when people mutually invest in each other over time, long-term mutual value will be created. The best referrals always come from the people who know you best, and the more time and history you have with someone, the closer you become in both life and business.

The call to talk to people and offer assistance is what opens the door to the conversation about getting their trigger events. Derek Coburn does this so he can introduce the idea of trigger events to his network. Once he can help them define their trigger phrases, he can be of service to him. This also naturally enables him to speak about these trigger phrases and offer them his. By educating them on how he can make better referrals to them, he is also able to make clear how they can do the same when an opportunity presents itself.

Coburn also schedules fifteen-minute interviews with really good clients and key people in his network and asks them a handful of questions. A big one: *What's the top challenge or opportunity you're focused on right now?*

"A lot of us have people in our network, or clients that we serve," he says. But we often don't know much about them. "We know they own an IT company, and that's about all we know," he says. "We don't know who they primarily provide their service for. What's the size of the company in terms of revenue or employees they like to target? If I have a key person in my network who runs an IT company providing tech services and I refer them to a company that has only twenty-five employees, yet the ideal minimum for their company is one hundred, then

I'm not adding value. I'm actually wasting their time. I'm doing worse than adding value."

Trigger Phrases and Trigger Events

This is the perfect opportunity for Coburn to educate them on how to get better referrals (which can help their businesses) as well as to share his own keywords. And since he is the person who first brought this to their attention, it's more likely that he'll remain top of mind.

The concept of "triggering events" stems from the term *trigger phrase*, which marketing expert John Jantsch discusses in his book *The Referral Engine*. What are trigger events or phrases? They are, essentially, the phrases that indicate someone may need your services at some point. "The easiest way to describe to someone what a trigger event or trigger phrase is by giving them examples from my own business," Coburn says. "What that does is help introduce them to this concept that I think will really help them and benefit them while they're out and about telling their key influencers and clients, 'Here's what you need to be on the lookout for when recommending people to me or referring people to me.'"

"An example of a trigger phrase for me is 'I have been managing my own money and don't have time to keep up with it,'" says Coburn. "Most people are not going to say, 'I need a great financial adviser' or 'I need an introduction to a financial adviser.' They may say, 'I am thinking about selling my business in a year.'" So that's one of the key phrases that he has people in his network pay attention to. He consistently reinforces these phrases with his network, so he remains top of mind.

A trigger phrase would reflect perhaps a triggering event, Coburn says. Perhaps something that has happened in life. For example, someone is getting ready to sell a business, which they tell you about six months before they even need you. "Figure out good triggering phrases for your business and then help your clients figure out triggering phrases to listen for in their own business," he says. "You can teach your clients how to do this by giving examples of what phrases you would be looking for. This also teaches the clients to listen for trigger phrases on your behalf. Even though the client interviews are for learning about your clients, you can teach clients and friends how to help you."

Creating a Frictionless Environment

Coburn holds customer-appreciation wine-tasting events. His events (and consequently his business) are all built on referrals, just like Jon Levy's dinners. Ditto for Jayson Gaignard, who gets thousands of inbound applications from people who want to attend his MastermindTalks. Guests are welcome to bring guests. In fact, he encourages them to do so—not in a creepy or insincere way, just as a way to meet new people.

This is all very deliberate. By being seen as the facilitator, and bringing in the right guests, natural conversations ensue. You know how it goes: if you've been invited to a high-quality event, you'll naturally ask the person who brought you certain questions: "What's this event about? Who's the host? How do you know him or her? What do they do?" These sorts of questions are likely to fuel positive responses, praise, and context-rich conversations that help your guest sell you without selling at all. There is no magic here—they're just talking as they normally would. But the framework of the environment is what makes this possible.

And this is all because Coburn set up the framework for the event correctly: creating the right environment, inviting the right group, making the right clear asks to hone the guest list, being viewed as the facilitator to establish credibility and authority, enabling clients to then speak about him and further establish his credibility and results, and finally creating moments to be brought into warm conversations and referrals. "If I'm investing my time and money into deepening existing relationships, especially if there's a recurring revenue place for my business, then it's still a great use of my time and money, even if I don't end up getting a new client or great new connection," he says. And it's never a bad thing to concentrate on your best relationships. The more you add value to their lives and provide guidance on trigger phrases and triggering events, the more likely you are to increase their desire to reciprocate.

Finally, you want to make sure people can easily get in touch with you online. If you've built strong Facebook forums or LinkedIn groups, or other digital communities, it's important to make sure people can easily get ahold of you. Make sure it's easy to contact you, whether via email, Facebook Messenger, or something else. Don't lose out on being recommended because your digital communities don't know how to connect with you in the real world.

We know, we know: social media can easily become a distraction, and for most it's a detractor from productivity.

Superconnectors, like all individuals online these days, need good rules in place to ensure that the time spent connecting with others online doesn't take away from time spent working or building your life . . . in real life.

We both have specific times during the day when we check and answer connections on social media. For example, Ryan spends about fifteen minutes in the morning scanning his feeds, answering messages, and looking for new opportunities while commuting into the office. The rest of the day, you'll rarely see him engaging with Facebook, LinkedIn, Twitter, or otherwise. These are his rules. It's up to you to come up with your own, so social media doesn't dominate your life.

How to Train Your Community to Refer the Right Opportunities Your Way

Like all of the people we interviewed for this book, Derek Coburn is really smart. He is so smart, in fact, that he has figured out a way that his anchors can sell him in a natural, nonsleazy, used-car-salesman kind of way on a regular basis. In effect, they are doing the work on his behalf.

In addition to being an author, Coburn also owns a wealth-management business and is the founder of Cadre, an "unnetworking" community in Washington, DC, that serves CEOs and business leaders. As mentioned, he also holds high-end customer-appreciation wine-tasting events. Coburn stresses that these events are *not* marketing events in disguise—he throws them truly to thank his clients, but he does give a ten- to fifteen-minute talk on a relevant financial topic.

Why do this? So people can put a face to the person throwing the extravaganza. So he can provide extra advice to his clients, and to demonstrate his expertise. His efforts have paid off.

During his first year holding these events, it was common for nearly 50 percent of his nonclients to reach out to him after the events. He generated nearly $150,000 in revenue, much of which came from people he encountered when they attended one of his events, people he most likely never would have otherwise met.

The Necessity of Team-Think Around the Importance of Connecting

Superconnectors build referrals into the fabric of what they do and the remarkable experiences they conduct.

But the "anchor effect," which we talked about earlier, also plays a role. You can extol your many virtues until those proverbial cows come home. But when someone else does it on your behalf, now you've arrived.

Paraag Marathe talks a lot about the importance of hiring connectors. By hiring and training connectors, you dramatically increase the number of smarter asks and referrals that benefit the whole. "More important than looking for bullet points on a résumé, you're looking for people with exceptional personal attributes because, again, it comes down to culture, and it comes down to when you know that the sum of the parts is much greater than the individual pieces," he says.

Superconnectors always have a simple and consistent ask, so it's easy to remember and to execute, and it works with word of mouth. In our case, it was always "If you know a phenomenal young entrepreneur we should know about for YEC, let us know."

At YEC we are constantly training the people around us in our belief system. Whether you're a business owner or climbing the corporate ladder, if you can share your beliefs with everyone and not just espouse niceties, you create magnets.

Let's go back to John Ruhlin, the gifting guru. His natural talent of giving gifts to others is so extraordinary—methodically, at scale—that he is able to attract referrals by staying top of mind with individuals who are just purely impressed (and he stokes the system by constantly investing part of the money he makes into his relationships, which only further fuels the engine).

Jim Pierce never saw any value in Chamber events from a "networking" perspective. As far as he was concerned, they were strictly for people with something to pitch and sell, which turned him off. "Most people go to networking events just to sell," he says. "They're not spending time developing a relationship with anyone. They're there to pass out business cards and calendars."

So what did he do? Instead of never returning, he turned the real estate on its head. Knowing that people who attended Chamber events were motivated to sell and make money, he decided to see who was best at it. He then asked them to sell for him and refer customers to him. This helped his business, built a relationship with new people, and turned what was largely a time waste into a value add—simply by applying his own rules to the real estate that was in front of him.

Indeed, one of the best feelings in the world is when someone thinks highly enough of you to recommend you for anything. It's like when someone wants to set you up on a blind date with one of their friends: if they didn't think well of you, they would never recommend you, right? It's someone else advertising you or your services, without your having to do a thing. The best Superconnectors know how to build their networks on referrals alone . . . just like we did with YEC. When people talk well about you, it's the ultimate compliment.

EPILOGUE
Superconnections

Over the years, we have both been fortunate to be mentored by truly amazing people, who have given us terrific advice. We often look back on some of the advice we've been given:

"Build a real business that makes real cash."

"Don't believe your own PR."

"Hire smarter people than you, but make sure they share your ethics and morals."

"You can't automate your humanity."

"It takes years to build your reputation and seconds to destroy it."

They're all quite profound. But nearly thirteen years later, one thing in particular has resonated, words of wisdom from one of Scott's mentors, Holly Peppe. "Real success," she told him, "takes real time." When he asked why, her response came swiftly: "Because you can't fake or cheat real time."

At that moment, Scott didn't fully appreciate how wise that simple sentence was. In fact (big shock), he barely even heard it. In typical Scott fashion, he started debating Holly and asking questions like "Well, how do I speed up progress? How can I get to point C faster without point B?"

"Holly was around captains of industry regularly—surely she knew how they did it better and faster," says Scott. "Surely she knew how they made their mark in half the time. But what she told me was even wiser, which I realized very quickly meant that the people who were trying to cheat or halve the time were actually the people fooling themselves and wasting their time. They weren't 'smarter' or 'more efficient.' They were fools. They were peddling fiction."

The smartest captains of industry realized quickly that you can't cheat time. So they maximized every minute to build the relationships that would ultimately define their lives and careers.

The true secret? That there *was* no secret. Most people don't believe this, which has allowed those who *do* get it to rise to the top.

We are surrounded by false messages, get-rich-quick schemes, and billion-dollar unicorn startups that promise the world. In our excitement, we forget that Santa Claus doesn't exist, there was no wizard in Oz, and there is no such thing as "overnight" success. Holly's simple statement has since informed every relationship Scott has made and every step he's taken as a businessman and connector. Every time he found himself wanting to push a boundary or trying to move something along faster, he would use Holly's words as a mantra to stop what he was doing, take a deep breath, and ask himself if he was being ambitious or reckless. This wasn't just in business, but in personal relationships, too.

If there's one thing we want you to take away from this book, it's that there isn't a magic formula or loophole to become successful at anything. You can't cheat real time; you can't hack relationships. You're cheating only yourself. And to cheat real time is to waste time, doing the very networking-type tasks we've been preaching against throughout this book. Whenever you try to do so—or, more precisely, every time you're told time can be defeated—take a deep breath and a giant step back.

But there is something else, too. As we noted, the genesis of "networking is dead" in part involves the arrival of social media, instant-gratification technology, and our twenty-first-century addiction to technology. You all know what we're talking about: that itch to check the number of "likes" you got on the photos you posted from your recent trip to the Grand Canyon. Or live-tweeting the last episode of *The Bachelor*, only to realize that you're devoting less energy to watching the show and are instead focused on reading and responding to your Twitter feed.

As with everything, if you do it in moderation, you're all good. But when these behaviors start taking precedence over the things happening IRL, then it's time for an intervention.

We want to urge you to utilize the same level of caution on your journey to becoming a Superconnector, because making connections is addictive. As you begin to develop these (dare we call them) superpowers, you will start seeing the world through new lenses. Where opportunity once was concealed, you'll start seeing it pop up where you least expect it. And like a newly drafted Pokémon GO player, you'll be yearning to catch 'em all.

As Adam Grant mentioned, both the most and the least successful people are givers. The defining factor that separates one from the other is boundaries, or knowing when to say no. Being able to set good boundaries as a Superconnector will drive success not only in your professional life but in your personal life as well.

We interviewed many Superconnectors for this book. Each one put heavy weight on how important their personal, untethered time was. Whether that was time with family and significant others, indulging in independent films, or camping in the wilderness, these moments of separation from the Superconnector lifestyle are what kept them grounded to the world and what's really important in life.

"I've seen what can happen when the Superconnector part of my life bubbles into the areas of my life where I spend time with the people that I cherish the most: my wife, my kids, my parents, my friends," says Ryan. "At times, checking my phone was like taking a breath. During family dinners, while watching cartoons with my kids, while having a beer with my best buddies at the bar, the endless opportunity at the tip of my fingers became an addiction." He even remembers certain holidays where he'd sneak off to the bathroom to check his emails. And then he realized that this was not productive to his well-being.

How did Ryan change? By putting his phone out of reach when he got home from work, a simple strategy that anyone can do but that all too often nobody does. He started telling himself, "This can wait until tomorrow"—which again, in our fast-paced world, many of us choose to forget. Even though it can!

He even began embracing a more minimalist lifestyle to offset the overabundance that the life of a Superconnector can sometimes create. Less stuff in his home, fewer planned activities (and more spontaneity). He is now in the process of buying a travel van so his family can spend time together off the grid, distraction free.

The moral is this: Being a Superconnector is a wonderful way to live that will connect you to people and opportunities that you never imagined. But it will never be more rewarding or impactful than the relationships right in front of you. It will never take the place of the people who love you for you, whether you're a Superconnector or not.

We believe that the best Superconnectors, the ones who truly succeed, first invest in and embrace the relationships that already matter in their lives: families, friends, colleagues, neighbors. The health of those relationships is a more important measure of success than anything you could take from the chapters in this book. Because it's only through these relationships that you'll truly be able to enjoy the profit that comes from being a great connector.

A Superconnector.

LIST OF SUPERCONNECTORS

Anjula Acharia, partner, Trinity Ventures

Patrick Ambron, CEO and cofounder, BrandYourself

Ryan Bethea, marketing and evangelism, Shoutpoint, Inc.

Abby Binder, LLC, owner/president/CEO, Abby Windows

Elliott Bisnow, founder and co-owner, Summit and Powder Mountain

Darrah Brustein, founder and co-CEO, Network Under 40

Susan Cain, cofounder and chief revolutionary, Quiet Revolution, best-selling author of *Quiet*

Derek Coburn, CEO and cofounder, Cadre

David Cohen, cofounder and co-CEO, Techstars

Erica Dhawan, CEO, Cotential

Jason Dorsey, president, Gen HQ

Michael Ellsberg, author of *The Education of Millionaires: It's Not What You Think and It's Not Too Late*

Allison Esposito, founder, Tech Ladies

Jeremy Fiance, founder and managing partner, The House Fund

Darius Foroux, author and founder, Procrastinate Zero

Jayson Gaignard, MastermindTalks, author of *Mastermind Dinners*, talent scout and curator, host of *The MMT Podcast*

Caleb Gardner

Adam Grant, Wharton professor and author of *Originals* and *Give and Take*

David Hassell, CEO, 15Five

Lewis Howes, founder of Sports Executives Association, author, entrepreneur, and former professional Arena League football player

Mitch Kanner, CEO, 2 Degrees Ventures

Erica Keswin, workplace strategist, founder of the Spaghetti Project

Pete Kistler, cofounder, head of product and lead designer, BrandYourself

Jared Kleinert, founder and author, *3 Billion Under 30*

Jon Levy

Paraag Marathe, chief strategy officer and executive vice president of football operations, San Francisco 49ers

Ryan D. Matzner, cofounder, Fueled

Jim Pierce, partner, Pierce & Bowen CPAs

Adam Rifkin, founder, PandaWhale

Michael Roderick, CEO, Small Pond Enterprises

Linda Rottenberg, cofounder and CEO, Endeavor

John Ruhlin, founder and CEO, Ruhlin Group

Dan Schawbel, *New York Times* best-selling author,
  Forbes and *Inc.* "30 Under 30," Fortune 500 con-
  sultant, serial entrepreneur, partner and research
  director of Future Workplace
Steve Sims, founder, The Bluefish
Shane Snow, author and cofounder, Contently
David Spinks, CEO, CMX Media
Rob Toomey, president, TypeCoach
Laurel Touby, journalist and investor, founder of
  Media Bistro
Ingrid Vanderveldt, EBW2020 and founder and chair-
  man, Vanderveldt Global Investments
Vanessa Van Edwards, behavioral investigator and
  author of *Science of People*
Mahesh Viswanathan, founder and inventor,
  LeakSpotter

NOTES

Unless otherwise noted, all of the interviews in this book were conducted by either Scott or Ryan.

Chapter 2

Amy Cuddy is a social psychologist at Harvard Business School and the author of the book *Presence*. She found that the strongest influences that we have on one another derive from a person's *perceived* warmth and competence.

A. J. C. Cuddy, S. T. Fiske, and P. Glick, "Warmth and Competence as Universal Dimensions of Social Perception: The Stereotype Content Model and the BIAS Map," *Advances in Experimental Social Psychology* 40 (2008): 61–149.

Chapter 3

The concept of EI was coined by researchers Peter Salovey and John D. Mayer, who described it as "the subset of social intelligence that involves the ability to monitor one's own and others' feelings and emotions, to discriminate among them and to use this information to guide one's thinking and actions."

Peter Salovey, Marc A. Brackett, and John D. Mayer, eds., *Emotional Intelligence: Key Readings on the Mayer and Salovey*

Model (Naples, FL: National Professional Resources/Dude, 2004).

Chapter 5

Keith Ferrazzi's story on meeting Hillary Clinton was published in "How I Avoided the Receiving Line and Met Hillary Clinton," LinkedIn, May 1, 2015, https://www.linkedin .com/pulse/how-i-avoided-receiving-line-met-hillary-clinton -keith-ferrazzi.

Chapter 6

Adam Rifkin swears by the "Five-Minute Favor."

"Panda Notes on Happiness and Meaning," LinkedIn, January 11, 2017, https://www.linkedin.com/pulse/panda-notes -happiness-meaning-adam-rifkin.

Chapter 13

One billion names are Googled every day. And 75 percent of human resource departments are *required* to research a candidate online before making a hire. Seventy percent of them have rejected candidates based on information they found online, while 85 percent say positive information has influenced them to make a hire.

"Why It Matters: Bad Results Hurt, and Good Results Help," https://brandyourself.com/info/about/whyCare.

Everything we do is now recorded online forever, which means we need more tools to make sure this doesn't harm us, according to Patrick Ambron.

"Online Reputation Management: The Ultimate Guide," https://brandyourself.com/online-reputation-management.

Chapter 16

Gary Vaynerchuk, a best-selling author, angel investor, and the CEO of VaynerMedia, believes that people should always decide what type of content would best fit *their* skill sets. If you are better verbally than on paper, then you might want to think about a podcast.

"Content Is King, but Context Is God," https://www.gary vaynerchuk.com/content-is-king-but-context-is-god/.

Chapter 17

A 2008 study in the *American Journal of Public Health* found that strong social ties might actually promote brain health.

Karen A. Ertel, M. Maria Glymour, and Lisa F. Berkman, "Effects of Social Integration on Preserving Memory Function in a Nationally Representative US Elderly Population," *American Journal of Public Health* 98, no. 7 (2008): 1215–1220.

ACKNOWLEDGMENTS

We would like to thank our wives, Tana and Caitlin; our children, Dalia, Aiden, Easton, Landon, JoJo, and Fisher; our awesome editors, Abby Ellin and Dan Ambrosio; and our The Community Company team for all of their love and support. Special shout-outs to our assistants, Stephanie Giron and Kiri Herrera, for organizing our lives so we don't have to. We couldn't have written this book without all of you in our corner.

And we are especially grateful to the amazing experts and Superconnectors who were gracious enough to share their expertise with us: Anjula Acharia, Patrick Ambron, Ryan Bethea, Abby Binder, Elliott Bisnow, Darrah Brustein, Susan Cain, Derek Coburn, David Cohen, Erica Dhawan, Jason Dorsey, Michael Ellsberg, Allison Esposito, Jeremy Fiance, Darius Foroux, Jayson Gaignard, Caleb Gardner, Adam Grant, David Hassell, Lewis Howes, Mitch Kanner, Erica Keswin, Pete Kistler, Jared Kleinert, Jon Levy, Paraag Marathe, Ryan D. Matzner, Jim Pierce, Adam Rifkin, Michael Roderick, Linda Rottenberg, John Ruhlin, Dan Schawbel, Steve Sims, Shane Snow, David Spinks, Rob Toomey, Laurel Touby, Ingrid Vanderveldt, Vanessa Van Edwards, and Mahesh Viswanathan.

INDEX

ABOUT THE AUTHORS

Scott Gerber is founder and CEO of The Community Company. He is an industry leader in building and managing personalized, invitation-only communities for world-class executives, entrepreneurs, and professionals. The Community Company is the team behind professional communities such as YEC, an invitation-only organization composed of more than fifteen hundred of the world's most successful young entrepreneurs founded by Scott, and Forbes Councils, a collective of invitation-only organizations for chief executives.

Scott is a sought-after public speaker, internationally syndicated business columnist, television commentator, author of the book *Never Get a "Real" Job*, and a special adviser to Forbes Media.

He has been widely recognized as the world's most syndicated columnist on the subject of millennial entrepreneurs and entrepreneurship. His columns appear regularly on or in *Time*, CNBC, CNN, Mashable, the *Next Web*, and *Huffington Post*. Scott is also a regular contributor to MSNBC, Fox Business, and CNN.

He has been a featured speaker at the White House and has rung the NASDAQ stock market closing bell. In 2011 he was named one of Mashable's "4 Young Social Good Entrepreneurs to Watch." In 2012 he was named a "Generation Y employment champion" by *Fortune*. In 2012 *Forbes* named his organization Young Entrepreneur Council as "America's most elite entrepreneur organization." In 2013 Fast Company named him a "Superconnector" and the "Pandora of Gen Y networking."

He has been featured on or in the *New York Times*, the *Wall Street Journal*, the *Washington Post*, *Time*, CNN, Reuters, Mashable, *CBS Evening News*, *ABC World News Tonight*, MSNBC, *US News & World Report*, Fox News, and *Entrepreneur*.

He lives with his wife and four children in New York City.

Ryan Paugh has been at the forefront of building highly curated, technology-enabled communities for ambitious professionals. He first cofounded Brazen Careerist, a career-management site for high-achieving young professionals and ambitious college students, where he led the company's community development efforts. Brazen Careerist was recognized as one of the top social networks for Gen Y entrepreneurs by Mashable.

Ryan then went on to cofound Young Entrepreneur Council in 2010 with Scott Gerber, an invitation-only organization for top entrepreneurs forty and under that *Entrepreneur* noted "has quickly become one of the most elite organizations of its kind." He saw YEC as a unique opportunity to apply the expertise he developed at Brazen Careerist to help fellow entrepreneurs access the resources, technology, and, most important, people they need to succeed. YEC's members now generate billions of dollars in revenue and have created tens of thousands of jobs.

Today, Ryan and his team are building on their vision of the future of professional organizations with The Community Company, a company poised to launch dozens of vetted communities engineered to help ambitious professionals grow their networks and expand their business opportunities. It's a mission Ryan identifies with; after graduating from Penn State University and launching his own entrepreneurial career, he knows firsthand the value of a trusted community.

Called "a cult legend in the online-community building world" by Mashable, Ryan is now focused on creating a strong membership experience and positive business outcomes for thousands of successful executives, thought leaders, business owners, and entrepreneurs across the country.

He lives with his family in Quincy, Massachusetts.

BONUS! We want to hear from you! Hit us up on Twitter @scottgerber and @ryanpaugh. Or visit us at Superconnectorbook.com.